HOW EMOTIONALLY DAMAGED ARE WE?

DISCOVER THE THINKIATRY®PRINCIPLES

And Learn the Self-Help Principles, Process, and Path to Healthier Psychological Functioning and Happiness Each Day.

JOHN LINDSAY O'BRIEN, Ph.D.

www.thinkiatry.com

Outskirts Press, Inc.
Denver, Colorado

To Alice:

My friend, my love, my wife, my life!

The only thing worse than not reading a book in the last ninety days – is not reading a book in the last ninety days and thinking it doesn't matter. – Jim Rohn

Contents

Part One: Discover The Principles

Part Two:
APPLYING THINKIATRY'S PRINCIPLES

INTRODUCTION

All that you achieve and all that you fail to achieve is the direct result of your own thoughts. **– James Allen**

This book, perhaps like no other book on a non-religious subject, has been written to be shared; to read, discuss, learn, and practice together with someone special in your life, such as your spouse, partner, significant other, friends, co-workers, siblings, son, daughter, etc. You will find, as I have, that you can attempt to explain Thinkiatry's principles and process until you are blue in the face; most people will nod their heads and say that it sounds very interesting, but unless they experience Thinkiatry with another person, the principles may never become a part of their life. Healthy psychological functioning and happiness may elude them forever. So, if there's someone else you really care about, buy a second copy. In fact, buy a third; you will always run into someone who needs a helpful self-therapy gift.

THINKIATRY? Think what? How do you spell that? OK, "think" and then what? "i-a-t-r-y!" "i-a-t-r-y?" Yes, that's it, "Thinkiatry." These are the usual responses I receive when discussing the newly trademarked name for the field of study I have created to teach the self-therapy principles, process, and path for people to achieve healthier psychological functioning and happiness in their lives and relationships each day.

Before we go any further, let's discuss something that most of us have never really thought about, much less attended any formal training for: the fact that all of us think 24/7, but very few of us know how or why our thinking, feelings, and resulting emotions work.

Like our breathing and heartbeat, thinking is something all of us do, but rarely do we think about how or why, or about the impact our thought process has upon our emotions and physical health. We don't really know all the answers. We do know that our breathing and heartbeat sustain our lives and make our thinking biologically possible. But our thinking determines the emotional quality and the resulting course of our lives each moment of each day we are alive.

Wait a minute! "Our thinking determines the emotional quality and the resulting course of our lives each moment of each day we are alive?"

If the way people think is that critical in determining the emotional quality of billions of people's lives, why don't more people know? Why isn't the way we think an integral part of our educational system's curriculum? Why have I experienced about 20 years of formal education without learning the way my thoughts and resulting emotions work? Why do so many people, even those with advanced educations, suffer from stress, anxiety, fear, depression, and so on? Why do about half of marriages end in divorce? How healthy is the thinking and resulting emotions of millions of children from broken families? How well can they perform in school and relationships when their habitual dysfunctional thinking controls their emotional lives?

Thinkiatry's Principles and My Happier Life

Thinkiatry's principles and processes are the result of

more than 30 years of my personal struggle to find more happiness and contentment in my life each day.

After several years of study and practice, my emotional life has changed dramatically, as I have used Thinkiatry's principles and process many times each day to ensure my own healthy psychological functioning and happiness.

As I became a confident Thinkiatrist (a disciple of Thinkiatry) I spent more than two years observing countless others in their daily behavior and relationships. I concluded that most of us have become victims, as I did, of their own unique, habitual thought systems—systems that allow the negative thoughts and opinions we have accumulated throughout our lives to control most of our thinking, emotional health, physical health, and level of happiness each day.

How many generally unhappy people do you encounter each day at work, at home, while shopping, while driving, on the nightly news, and so on? Yet Thinkiatry's principles and process have proven that our level of happiness lies hidden beneath our generally accepted, "just the way life is," chronic, habitual, negative thinking.

Thinkiatry's first principle is the principle of thinking, the way we think. This principle taught me several things I had, like you, never considered or even thought about. First, contrary to popular belief, my thoughts are not real unless I choose to make them real. A perfect example involves stress. Stress does not really exist, but stressful thinking does, and it creates our emotional distress. In my opinion, stress is merely a socially accepted form of mental dysfunction that "stressed out" people create within their own minds and truly believe is real.

Second, I learned that I could actually **"watch what I think"** and choose which thoughts to follow and which to let fade away to my mental trash bin because they were negative. Negative thoughts serve no useful purpose in our lives but lead to all known forms of human emotional distress.

Thinkiatry's second principle is feelings. I learned that my feelings are a navigational tool that let me know if my thinking is getting off track. If I allow negative thoughts to pass my first line of thinking defense, I instantly feel the effects, and I am reminded that negative thoughts will only lead to distress and **Thinkiatry's third principle, moods.** With practice, I have virtually eliminated mood swings; because I typically never let negative thoughts get past my feelings, low moods now only rarely occur.

For years, the relationships in my life were troubled and were sources of frustration, low self-esteem, and disappointment. I had no control over my negative thinking, I stuttered, and I felt rejected when others did not agree with me or shunned my thinking. My stuttering and low self-esteem compounded my negative thinking and resulting emotions. **Thinkiatry's fourth principle, separate realities,** taught me that each of us has our own unique reality comprised of thoughts, experience, and opinions that have accumulated throughout our lives. No two people can possibly think the same way and, as you will learn, that's OK.

This principle has taught me not to expect others to think like I do. I now appreciate and respect another's unique separate reality leading to interesting and more meaningful relationships with my wife of 30 years, my four grown children, four and soon to be five grandchildren, extended family, coworkers, and others I meet each day.

Thinkiatry's first four self-therapy principles now allow me to eliminate virtually all of my habitual negative thinking each day. Without negative thoughts, anxiety, stress, depression, and so on cannot exist, and my emotional life has changed dramatically. My happiness is no longer buried beneath years' worth of chronic negative thoughts and the emotional distress they create.

Without negative thoughts and the accompanying drama surrounding relationships, I am free to be happy and content most of the time. The first four principles have prepared me to achieve one of life's most important spiritual goals and

Thinkiatry's fifth principle, life in the moment.

On a scale of one to ten, what do you think the average level of happiness is among the world's inhabitants today? Among all the people you now know? How about you?

Most people have heard the expression "putting the cart before the horse." If the habitual way we think is the root of our emotional health, and if few of us know how to achieve healthy psychological functioning and happiness, what are the odds of ever reaching our human potential or sustained happiness in our lives? The odds aren't good. Our level of happiness and contentment in our lives lies hidden within each of our unique habitual thought processes which have been developing since birth.

Our Habitual Thinking

The way we currently think is controlled by our habitual thought systems, which begin to form in early childhood. It has been said that we learn approximately 90% of what we will ever learn in the first five years of our lives. Our thinking is determined by the input from and perceptions of our parents, siblings, family, friends, environment, religion, mass media, and so on.

We learn how to be angry, jealous, greedy, selfish, etc. We also learn how to laugh, cry, and manipulate others, how to be good, and how to be bad. By the time we start our school years, the foundations for our own totally unique habitual thought system have been laid.

Attending school further exposes us to the wonderful world of relationships. We find that we like some classmates and dislike others. We discover that the way another's habitual thought system works can have a serious impact on the way we feel each day. Today, bullying, racial and sexual profiling, and many other dysfunctional habitual thoughts cause daily emotional crises and confrontations in our schools and in the workplace.

In our teens, most of us really begin to think and instantly feel the multitude of emotions our untrained habitual thought systems continuously create. We fight depression, anxiety, relentless peer pressure, insecurity, low self-esteem, and on and on.

By the time we are young adults, many people question whether to continue their education as well as the value of formal education, because to most, the educational process is not fun. Today, many students question the value of their curriculums, imposed by government agencies, administrators, and teachers. They want to learn how to buy a car, a home; they can see the value of balancing a checking account, but don't believe they will ever use advanced algebra or statistics. Many feel life will be better if they fall in love, get married, and have a child and a family. How prepared are these young adults to meet adult life challenges?

Today, our habitual thinking is overwhelmed by our political systems, financial systems, world religions, Wall Street, corporations, unemployment rates, failing housing markets, and mega-media, instant-information technology. Our high levels of emotional distress, insecurity, fear, and unhappiness are historically unprecedented.

Why can't we all just get along and be happy? Why are so many people unhappy and, typically, emotionally consumed by their perceived circumstances, relationship problems, and generally unhappy lives? Learning Thinkiatry's principles and process will teach you that simplicity is genius. The only things standing between us and our living a healthier, happier, more content, more prosperous life are the way we have learned to think and the total control our habitual thought systems have over our emotional lives.

Today, our habitual thought systems are typically dominated by varying levels of negative thoughts. We rarely, if ever, consciously think about this fact. Test yourself by committing to tally the approximate number of negative thoughts you feel in one day—don't worry about counting your dreams.

You're thinking, "OK, I do have some level of negative thoughts every day. So what? Everybody does. It's just the way life is, and we have to deal with it, like we always have." That statement defines the root of the problem and the challenge most of us have to overcome in order to achieve healthier psychological functioning and happiness; we have been conditioned to accept the situation as "just the way life is" and tolerate our negative-thinking emotional rollercoaster.

Negative Habitual Thinking—The Price We Pay

Negative thoughts serve no useful purpose in our lives! That statement may shock you. It is blatantly simple and will ultimately lead countless others, including myself, to exclaim, "Why didn't I learn how my negative habitual thinking and Thinkiatry's principles work years ago? It would have dramatically altered the emotional quality of my relationship with my own thinking, my relationships with others, and possibly the course of my life."

When we think about our emotional health, we normally speak in terms such as I'm depressed, I feel sad, I have too much stress, my anxiety is overwhelming me, I really fear my marriage is falling apart, and so on.

Well, Thinkiatry's principles teach us that we cannot feel depressed without depressing thoughts, we can't be sad without sad thoughts, feel stressed without stressful thoughts, suffer from anxiety without anxious thoughts, and so on.

What happens to these very common human emotions if Thinkiatry's principles teach you that our thoughts are not real? If we learn that we can choose which thoughts become our perceived realities and that we can virtually eliminate dysfunctional negative thinking from our lives each day? Again, genius is simplicity. Every category of human emotional distress starts with a single negative thought, which we assume is real because otherwise we wouldn't have had the thought. When we learn that only we make our thoughts reality, we can use Thinkiatry's principles to dismiss negative thoughts anytime we decide to do so—usually many times each day.

Here is the inspiring bottom line. We no longer have to accept our habitual negative thinking as "just the way life is." Learning Thinkiatry's principles literally chang-es the emotional playing field and allows you to win by passively ignoring as many negative thoughts as you can. Eliminating habitual negative thinking and moving it to our minds' trash bins has the potential to virtually elimi-nate depression, sadness, stress, anxiety, and so on from our lives each day. Without the negative thought, the re-sulting emotion can't exist!

Thinkiatry and Our Habitual Thinking Process

I have not been able to find any definitive scientific source, but the best source I could find estimates that the average person has approximately 50,000 thoughts each day. To my knowledge, we don't know where our thoughts come from, but like our heartbeat and our breathing, they are simply functions of being alive. That's 18,250,000 thoughts per year, on average.

Multiply that by your age, and the result equals your average total lifetime thoughts; hundreds of millions of thoughts that create your unique life perceptions, experiences, emotions, and the perceived reality that we call our habitual thinking processes.

When was the last time you thought about how you think? Probably never. Why don't we think about the way we think? Well, for one thing, because no one has ever given us a reason to; that's why Thinkiatry's principles and process have been created—to teach people that the key to healthy psychological functioning and happiness in their lives lies hidden within the way they habitually think.

The good news is that you have the opportunity, in order to achieve your life's highest level of mental health and happiness, to learn how to use Thinkiatry's principles and process to monitor and manage your habitual thinking.

We now have a choice. You may stay where you are in your dysfunctional, habitual-thinking comfort zone and live with your own unique level of emotional distress each day, or you can begin to make Thinkiatry's principles and process a part of your life by learning the skills and gaining the knowledge required to change the emotional landscape of your life for the better, forever.

Thinkiatry's five principles will teach you how we think and why habitual negative thoughts are responsible for the high levels of stress, anxiety, anger, depression, and so on in our society today; how our feelings and subsequent moods are created by the way we think; and how understanding the separate realities principle will unlock relationship quality you never thought possible. Finally, you will learn the process for achieving the elusive and prized life in the moment, in which happiness and contentment are the only menu options.

The remaining chapters will teach you how to apply Thinkiatry's principles to several of life's typical emotional challenges: relationships, stress, habits and addictions, solving life problems, happiness, obesity, parenting, and much more.

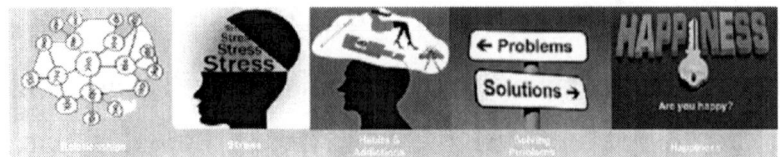

Clearly now, our habitual negative thoughts lie at the root of all human emotional distress. So, how do we begin to learn to manage and control our thinking? Not by trying to create positive thinking in order to find happiness; this age-old suggestion and technique simply gives us the opportunity to fail. How do you think positively while your habitual thinking is invariably negative? And then how do you feel when your attempts to positively think your way to happiness are unsuccessful.

On the contrary, Thinkiatry's first three principles—thinking, feelings, and moods—teach us that the key to happiness in our lives is in the knowledge and skills the principles reveal in order to virtually eliminate our habitual negatives. Without the influence of chronic negative thoughts, you'll be amazed how often you'll feel healthier psychological functioning and true happiness in your life each day. The key to happiness and contentment in life lies not in our circumstances, not in having lots of money, a big house, fancy cars, and not in who you know, but, quite simply, it is in using Thinkiatry's principles and process to eliminate as many habitual negative thoughts and their resulting emotions as possible.

For many years I have professed that each of our lives is a journey comprised of many chapters, much like a book. Therefore, I now congratulate you! You have just completed the Introduction to Thinkiatry, the next chapter in your life's journey.

Our next step is Part One, discovering Thinkiatry's five principles, beginning with the way we **THINK**, and how to change, manage, control, and virtually eliminate our habitual negative thoughts and their resulting emotional distress from our lives each day.

Part One:
DISCOVER THE PRINCIPLES

Thinking

Feelings

Moods

Separate Realities

The Present Moment

Principle #1:
THINKING

As thoughts enter our consciousness, we have a choice:
We can look at them and respond, or simply let them go.
– John O'Brien

Understanding the principle of thought and how we think is the foundation for healthier psychological functioning and a happier life each day. We humans are thinking creatures. Each moment of each day we are thinking in order to make sense out of what we see and experience.

Thinking is an ability we all have—a function of our human consciousness. As is true with other human functions, such as our heartbeat or breathing, thinking is constant, whether we want it to be or not. Yet we are the producers of our own thinking. Thought is not something that happens to us, but something that we do. Contrary to popular belief, it comes from our minds' habitual thinking processes, not from outside circumstances. What we habitually think determines how we interpret what we see—not vice versa, as most of us would assume.

We have all spent our entire lives creating and nurturing our own totally unique habitual thought system. How you have perceived and interpreted your life experience has molded the way you think. No two thought systems are identical, and other people will never think the same way you do.

This truth is the primary reason our most troubled relationships are usually with those closest to us. The more time we spend with someone, the more obvious our differences in thinking become. Most of us expect others to think as we do. In fact, many initial friendships are formed when two people think they have found a common thinking bond. It does not take long for us to realize that we will always have our differences. We will discuss our relationships with others in a later chapter in which we discuss the fourth principle, separate realities.

Thinkiatry's most basic hypothesis is that our current thinking is a slave to our habitual thought system, which contains all of the negative thoughts we have accumulated while living our lives. These negative thoughts surface throughout the minutes and hours of each day.

The best information I could find estimates that the average person has about 50,000 thoughts every day. Logically, those with a higher level of emotional distress will be plagued by a higher level of negative thinking. Those who consider themselves emotionally healthy and happy will have fewer habitual negative thoughts. However, none of us are immune. Over time, we all have life experiences that make us sad, angry, hopeless, depressed, and so on. Thinkiatry's principles help us all every day, regardless of the frequency and severity of our emotional storms.

Negative thoughts serve no healthy purpose in our lives. If we eliminate negative thoughts, we eliminate stress, depression, anxiety, jealousy, and so on. Emotional distress can not exist without our habitual negative thoughts.

Just imagine learning the skills and gaining the knowledge required, and living each day with few, if any, negative thoughts and their emotional consequences. This sounds challenging, and there are a number of major hurdles we must individually overcome to even begin to accept, learn, and implement Thinkiatry's first principle.

The first obstacle is that many of us have never thought about the way we think, or, most important, how to "watch" what we think. We have no current concept of having a relationship with our own thinking. We have always thought and just assumed that our thoughts are reality. Left with no other choice, we have spent our lives trying to deal with the emotions our habitual negative thoughts create.

We assume that if we have a thought, it is reality for us and everybody else. As we will discuss later, both of these assumptions are absolutely wrong. Accepting the way we habitually think as "just the way life is" is hard to overcome because of a condition I call the normalcy bias. We all suffer from this bias to varying degrees.

The Normalcy Bias

It's very difficult for our species to try new things or to understand something that's completely different from our previous life experiences; I call this the normalcy bias. We all have difficulty with change and simply cannot conceive of ideas and practices that we think are too far outside what we perceive as "normal" or just the way life is. For many, it can be very difficult, even painful, to even try something new!

The normalcy bias has protected and enabled our negative habitual thinking and resultant emotional consequences for centuries.

Some people don't necessarily like to hear that there are principles and a process to change and to learn to achieve healthier psychological functioning and a happier life—it means commitment, study, practice, and work. Others like to hear and read about it, but their normalcy bias kicks in, and they don't take any action. It's easier to just continue yielding to our normalcy bias and doing what we have always done. So most of us *illogically* continue to allow our habitual thinking to control varying levels of unending emotional distress and turmoil in our lives and relationships each day.

I will say more about how I learned to overcome my normalcy bias in a few minutes. **Let's test yours.** The first way to challenge your normalcy bias is to learn to "watch what you think."

Learning to "Watch What You Think"

It may initially sound odd, but we need to begin to learn to "watch what we think." Don't worry if you are preoccupied and forget; Thinkiatry's second principle, feelings, which you'll learn about in our next chapter, will provide virtually foolproof backup guidance and serve as a navigational tool.

We have already established Thinkiatry's fundamental hypothesis: our habitual negative thinking results in all of the emotional distress in our lives. Further, the more negative thoughts we can train ourselves to choose to ignore and send to our mental trash bin each day, the fewer emotional consequences we will ever feel or become a victim of.

Without habitual negative thoughts, emotional distress such as anger, anxiety, fear, and depression cannot exist. Without these negative thoughts and their resultant emotional distress, your life begins to change immediately. Happiness and contentment become your daily norm quite quickly.

As you begin to watch your thoughts and choose your own reality, you will definitively understand that you really can choose which thoughts to pursue and which to ignore. You might be thinking, "How in the world do I learn to ignore bad thoughts such as anger, anxiety, jealousy, etc.?" It's not as hard as your normalcy bias may lead you to believe. But it does take some patience, discipline, practice, and effort.

"Switching Away" Habitual Negative Thoughts

You will undoubtedly develop your own methods, but when I get stuck thinking negatively, I may think about my love for Winchels, my cat. Winchels was my buddy and companion for about 15 years. We lost him to diabetes and cancer a few years ago. The minute I think about him, I smile and say "I miss you Winch." Any negative thought(s) I may have had instantly disappear, just as quickly as they came into my mind.

Another switch I may use is to think about my wife and about how very fortunate I am to have her in my life. As watching what you think becomes a part of your life, you will create your own negative thinking switches you can use to ignore the negative thoughts you will have each day.

Having lived Thinkiatry's principles now for more than two years, I have discovered that watching what I think has other inherent, ancillary benefits that I now consider very important. I have learned the value of slowing down my habitual thinking. When a questionable negative thought comes to mind, I create a watch-window pause. I take a few seconds to review the thought in my mind. I ask myself, does this thought make me feel good? If it doesn't, I immediately use my "switch" and ignore it, sending it to my trash bin.

At this moment, your normalcy bias may not allow you to understand the significance, value, or importance of the pause watching what you think creates. But I had no idea how the years I spent blurting out whatever negative thought I had each moment contributed to my emotional distress and how it affected my personality and my relationships. None of it had been positive, to say the least.

Again, our negative thoughts serve no useful purpose in our lives. Watching what we think is the first step to removing as many of these negatives as we possibly can. Just think about the positive impact reducing or eliminating your negative thinking can have each day. Little or no anxiety, anger, stress, depression . . .

I don't want you to think that watching what you think is like turning on a switch. Like any other change in your life, it may take some time, depending on how consumed with negative thoughts your habitual thinking has become. It will take work and lots of practice, but what price is too high for eliminating negative thoughts and emotions from your life each day?

Overcoming Your Normalcy Bias

How did your normalcy bias do with "watching what we think"? As stated previously, our normalcy bias makes it very difficult for our species to try new things or understand something that's completely different from our previous life experiences. We all have difficulty and simply cannot conceive of ideas and practices that we think are too far outside what we perceive as "normal" or just the way life is.

Learning Thinkiatry's five principles, and particularly this first, thinking principle, is certainly a complete change from our previous life experiences and will certainly threaten many readers' normalcy biases.

The normalcy bias is a real and unfortunate paradox forced by our habitual thought systems. After all, **change is life**. Our bodies and physical appearance change. Just take a look at your photo album. For many, our physical address has changed several times. Our jobs change. New relationships begin, while others fade away. But watching and altering our thought processes is a real stretch for many. They are simply content living their lives as they always have, allowing their habitual negative thoughts to control their emotional lives.

Although your unique habitual thinking is different than mine, we all face the same hurdle: overcoming our habitual thinking to free us from the negative thoughts that have controlled our emotions since childhood. Given this common ground, I will explain how I was able to overcome my normalcy bias.

We all have a life story, and I don't want to burden you with mine—perhaps in another book someday. But I will provide you with a brief background. For a number of reasons I grew up stuttering and had very low self-esteem. So my emotions became the focus of my life at about seven years of age. I was terrified of going to school each day, fearing I would be called on to speak or read.

As a teen, my emotional dysfunction began to impact every aspect of my life. Then, I won the only thing I have ever won in my life: my birthday was selected as number five in the Vietnam draft lottery in 1969. I married my childhood sweetheart, and she left me for another. I spent several years as a workaholic, burying my emotional pain in my work, as most of us do.

In my early thirties, my wife of now 30 years forced me out of my normalcy bias, and I began professional therapy and medication. Therapy lasted only a couple of years, because they wanted me to talk about all the negatives I had experienced. I left each session more confused, upset by all of my life's negatives I was counseled to bring back to the present moment and talk about. I felt hopeless and more depressed. Then I began a trial-and-error regimen of prescribed medications, each with their own side effects and complications. I just wanted to live a happy, normal life.

I lost confidence in modern psychology's therapy, whose strategy appeared to be to identify the negatives I had experienced in my life, bring them back to the forefront of my thinking, and then rehash them, bringing back endless emotional pain and even more negative thoughts, leading to frustration and hopelessness.

I spent the better part of 30 years reading, studying, and researching how our minds work, the way we think, and how our emotions are given life through our habitual thinking. One day about three years ago, I discovered several books written by Dr. Richard Carlson[*] author of *Don't Sweat the Small Stuff* and many other must-read books, and discovered the principles. The first four principles were originally formulated by Dr. Rick Suarez and Dr. Roger C. Mills.[**]

All my years of emotional struggle, study, and relentless pursuit of healthier psychological functioning and happiness gave me a unique level of insight and a profound understanding of both the importance of these principles and the process they created to help me and countless others change the emotional landscape of our lives.

Principle #1: The Way We Think—Summary

- Our habitual negative thoughts are the sole source of our ability to create emotional distress in our lives. Without a negative thought, it is not possible for any of us to feel stress, anxiety, insecurity, or any other emotional baggage.

---

[*]   Please visit www.richardcarlson.com in memoriam to learn more about his life and works.
[**]   Rick Suarez, Roger C. Mills, and Darlene Stewart, *Sanity, Insanity, and Common Sense: The Groundbreaking New Approach to Happiness* (New York: Fawcett, Columbine, 1987).

- Our life's happiness and contentment have lain buried beneath our habitual negative thinking for countless generations.

- Our normalcy bias is the single greatest challenge to changing and to learning Thinkiatry's principles, process, and path to healthier psychological functioning and happier lives.

- Watching what we think in order to eliminate negative thoughts and their resulting crippling emotions is the first tactic we must learn to become a Thinkiatrist, joining the happiest people on earth.

There are two other very important factors we will discuss in later chapters. First, both the known and unknown medical and physiological consequences our bodies endure because of stress, anxiety, anger, depression, and so on. What impact do our emotions have on the physical health of our bodies and on our life expectancies?

The second factor concerns the habits and addictions many people use as self-treatment for the emotional pain and misery their habitual negative thinking creates. In fact, like our happiness and contentment, I believe treating many of our habits and addictions requires switching away negative thoughts at the root of the addiction.

Let's move on to Thinkiatry's second principle, our **FEELINGS**—the foolproof navigational tool we will use to make sure we are always actively watching what we think and eliminating our habitual negative thoughts.

Principle # 2:
OUR FEELINGS

Our feelings tell us, with total accuracy, when our thinking is off track and headed toward emotional distress.
— John O'Brien

Thinkiatry's second principle, feelings, provides us with a foolproof guidance system to continually navigate our emotional path to a happier, more content life each day.

This system, which consists solely of our feelings, lets us immediately know when we are off track and headed toward unhappiness, conflict, and a low mood. Our feelings are a barometer, letting us know what our internal weather is like.

When we think, we immediately feel the effects of our thoughts. The amount of time it takes us to feel the effects of a thought is the same amount of time it takes to see light when we flip the switch; most of us aren't even aware that it's happening.

Two Examples of Our Thought to Feeling Speed

Please take a moment to test your thought to feeling speed:

- Think about the person or pet you probably love the most in your life. What thoughts first come to mind? How do these thoughts feel? This is how fast our thoughts affect our feelings to create a corresponding emotion. You can also feel your body's physical response to this good thought with a warm, content feeling.

- Now think about the person or thing you dislike the most in your life. This is the speed a single negative thought takes to affect the way you feel. What was your body's physical response? Fear, anger, anxiety, a knot in your stomach . . .

For most of you, this exercise is probably the first time you have been specifically exposed to the instant relationship between your thoughts and feelings. We will discuss how our habitual negative thinking affects our nervous system and physical health in a later chapter, entitled Habits and Addictions.

As you have now experienced, our feelings are to our mental health as the warning lights on our dashboards are to our automobiles. Warning lights tell us to direct our attention to the vehicle messages and operation; as our feelings turn negative, they tell us to pay immediate attention to our thinking.

Whenever our feelings begin to turn negative, toward anger, jealousy, insecurity, depression, or unhappiness in some way, we need to learn to understand that these feelings are being manufactured by our own thought system and are not accurate or representative of reality. The only value habitual negative feelings have is that they let us know that we are seeing life in a distorted, dysfunctional manner.

So what do we do when we feel angry, depressed, or anxious? How do we stop feeling these emotions and return to healthy psychological functioning? Trust and see the truth in Thinkiatry's principle of feelings. When we learn where our negative feelings come from, our habitual thinking, there is no need to defend or hang on to them. Negative feelings will disappear quickly enough when we learn to simply "switch away" the thought(s). There will be more about switching coming up. Negative feelings are created by our habitual thoughts—to focus on them or analyze them will only extend and deepen the negative emotions we are creating.

The Thinkiatry Process Begins

Our book's subtitle professes *And Learn the Self-Help Principles, Process, and Path . . .* and our process is now beginning to take shape. Our feelings are constantly reacting to our thoughts, good or bad.

As explained in the chapter on the thinking principle, there are times when watching what you think in order to switch away negative thoughts will become a challenge. But your feelings are always on the alert and can't miss. We can't have a thought without a resulting feeling.

Your feelings instantly react and alert your thinking and physical responses to tell you there is at least one habitual negative thought attempting to challenge Thinkiatry's process. One of two things will then happen. You will consciously decide to switch away the negative(s) and emotional stability will be restored, or you will be unable, or unwilling, to stop the habitual negative thinking. This will happen; there is no 100 percent cure. After all, we are dealing with negative emotions that if left unchecked will at times become pretty nasty. But, eventually, the feelings will fade away and we will start watching what we think again, with more conviction this time.

Thinkiatry's principles shed new light on the age-old question, "Did I hurt your feelings?" The emotional pain was not caused by another, but comes from within our own habitual negative thoughts, if we choose to allow our healthy psychological functioning to be overcome. We then make ourselves the victim and unhealthy emotional drama ensues.

Some people will use Thinkiatry's principles and process to virtually eliminate their negative thoughts, while others will provide little resistance. This fact deserves a pointed question and a brief discussion.

Why Some Will Choose To Do What They Have Always Done

Are there people who will subconsciously choose to live emotionally distressed lives, and why? The short answer is, of course there are. But why? The following are a few suggested reasons.

- Since childhood, we have all had to learn to cope with our habitual negative thinking. These folks have never had another option.
- Without another option and no formal education

regarding why they feel so emotionally distressed, some choose to do the best with the hand they have been dealt. They have learned how to use their emotional distress and ensuing drama to manipulate others.

- They want to be the center of attention and share their habitual-thought-created emotions with anyone who will listen, thus disrupting their relationships and causing untrained others to experience negative thoughts and lower morale as well. Most offices and other work environments have at least one of these personality types.

Although they are truly unhappy and insecure, they occupy their time and live their lives moving from one of their self-created emotional dramas to another, thinking that the way they are living their lives is just the way it is, the way everybody else does.

Encountering and dealing with people like those mentioned above, and other aspects of all of our relationships, will be discussed in Principle #4: Separate Realities, and applying Thinkiatry's principles to our relationships is a topic in Part Two.

Using Thinkiatry's principles and process, we are instantly alerted to any thought(s) creating a bad feeling. At this moment, we have to choose to switch the negative thinking away or allow ourselves to become a victim of our self-created habitual negative thought and ensuing emotions.

In my early experience making Thinkiatry's principles and process an integral part of my life every day, I did my best to switch away every negative thought and feeling I had. I was absolutely convinced that no negative thought was worth keeping. The results very quickly altered my emotional life. If I had to guess, I'd say I was able to eliminate about 80 percent of my life's daily emotional distress within the first few weeks.

I was amazed how the absence of my habitual negative thoughts and emotions changed the quality of my attitude, personality, relationships, and my life each day. I felt little or no stress, anxiety, frustration, depression, or other negative emotions. The time I used to spend dealing with the emotions my negative thinking had habitually created was then free to devote to feeling content and happy, improving job and relationship performance, and just plain feeling good. This state of being is called **healthy psychological functioning.**

Once we understand Thinkiatry's principles and their ability to lead us to healthy psychological functioning, we are no longer tempted to analyze or think our way to happiness. Happiness is already with us and always has been, buried beneath our habitual negative thinking.

This book will teach you, and countless others, the knowledge and skills to change the emotional landscape of your life for the better, forever. Become a Thinkiatrist, and join the happiest people on earth.

Thinkiatry Principle #2: FEELING—Summary

- Our feelings provide us with a foolproof guidance system to continually navigate our emotional path to a happier, more content life each day.
- Our feelings are a barometer, letting us know what our internal weather is like.
- The only value our habitual negative feelings have is that they let us know that we are seeing life in a distorted, dysfunctional manner.
- Your feelings and physical responses instantly react and alert your thinking to the fact that there is at least one habitual negative thought attempting to challenge Thinkiatry's process.

If our habitual negative thoughts go unchecked, our bad feelings and emotions continue to grow, usually at a fast, or even exponential, rate, sometimes called "thought attacks." We become overwhelmed by the negative emotions we have created, resulting in Thinkiatry's third principle and our next chapter—**MOODS**.

Principle #3:
MOODS

3RD PRINCIPLE

Moods

When we understand the power our moods have on our perspective, we will no longer need to react to or become victims of them. – John O'Brien

We all have them. The only variables are their frequency and degree. Where do they come from? Why do they happen? Is there a way to reduce their emotional impact or virtually eliminate the bad ones?

Highs and Lows

When we are in a high or good mood, Thinkiatry's thinking and feelings principles and processes are doing their job. We are successfully switching away any habitual negative thoughts we may think or feel and are joyfully experiencing our own unique healthy psychological functioning. Life looks and feels good. In our high moods, things don't feel so difficult, problems are easier to solve and seem less insurmountable. In good moods, communication is easy and enjoyable; our relationships are healthy and often fun.

Conversely, in our low moods we have momentarily lost our constant battle with our habitual negative thoughts. For any number of personal reasons, usually because we start to blame our life circumstances rather than our habitual negative thinking, we have regressed and our negative thoughts and feelings are in charge. It's never too late to recover our healthy psychological functioning, but it is very difficult to stop the momentum the negative thoughts and feelings have gained. Odds are you are on your way to a bad or low mood.

In low moods, just about everything in life looks very serious and difficult. We lose our perspective; we feel that others are out to get us, or that they don't care about our problems and emotional distress—the problems and emotions that we have created with our now unchecked habitual negative thoughts. Life seems to be all about us. We take things personally and often negatively misinterpret those around us.

These characteristics of moods are true for everyone. No one is happy or fun to be around when in a low mood, or unhappy, defensive, or angry in a high mood.

The goals of Thinkiatry's principles are to provide us with the knowledge, skills, and process to virtually eliminate negative habitual thoughts, allowing us to experience healthy psychological functioning and happiness most of the time. However, we are all human, and there will be times in all of our lives that negative thinking and the resultant feelings will defy and overcome our best intentions and effort.

Understanding Our Moods

By understanding the moods principle, we learn to be appreciative of our good moods and more graceful in our lows. This totally differs with what most of us currently do in a low mood; our instinct is to try to impatiently think and force our way out of it. But we can't force our way out of a low mood any more than we can force ourselves to have a good time doing something we don't like.

Even worse, because life feels so serious in a low mood,

we feel a sense of urgency to try to feel better. This is why so many people try to have their serious discussions in low moods, and it is one of the core problems in marriages and relationships. Many serious relationship problems turn out to be nothing more than two people who have made a habit of taking each other's low moods too seriously.

With a better understanding of how and why we have low moods as well as the power they have on our perspective, we will no longer need to continue any negative thought attacks or become victims of them. We will become more graceful and patient with our lows and return to a state of healthy functioning sooner with less emotional damage to ourselves and others.

Everything seems to appear differently in different moods. As we begin to understand this Thinkiatry principle, our compassion for ourselves and others increases dramatically. We will now know that at times our partners, friends, and others will see the upside or opportunity in a situation, and at other times they will only see the dark downside. When we learn to recognize other people's moods, we will cease to judge them with negative thoughts and feelings when they are seeing the darker side of life.

Low moods are a distortion in our thinking. In my own experience, after incorporating Thinkiatry's principles into my life each day for a couple of years now, I rarely experience low moods anymore. You will become very good at using the first two principles to switch away negative thoughts that you think or feel. Without an accumulation of compounding habitual negative thoughts and feelings, low moods just don't happen much anymore. Like our many conditions of emotional distress, if we are successful using Thinkiatry's first two principles, eliminating virtually all negatives, our low moods can't exist unless something really tragic happens in our life.

Low Moods: Helpful Tips

I can offer a few additional ideas and suggestions, based upon both my personal moods and experience with others, to help you further understand the moods principle.

- Your moods change, but not your life. It is your mood, not your life, that has suddenly changed.
- Don't take yours or another's low mood too seriously. Give yourself a break and focus on eliminating the negative thoughts you allowed to create the low mood.
- Leave your low-mood partner or other party alone; so often, just a little time alone is all they need to pull themselves out of it.
- The last thing a person with a low mood needs is to be questioned or argued with. Most people in

relationships don't give each other the space they need in a low mood.

- Don't try to solve your problems while in a low mood. Your emotions in a low mood will have you convinced your negative thoughts and feelings are real; they are bad mood feelings and are not your true feelings. The problem(s) will still be there after your low mood has subsided. After your healthy psychological functioning has returned, you will have access to your problem-solving healthy thoughts and wisdom.

- Finally, unless you have no other choice, do not confront someone while you (or they) are in a low mood; we can be assured of the result. One or both of you will likely become defensive, annoyed, angry, and so on.

Thinkiatry's first three principles are interwoven and create the process that enables us to eliminate as many of our habitual negative thoughts as possible, because negative thoughts serve no useful purpose in our lives. These thoughts are the root of all negative, mentally and physically destructive emotions we experience.

Working as a process, the principles teach us by learning the skills and gaining the knowledge required to overcome our lifelong habitual negative thinking and the crippling emotional consequences many of us experience more than once everyday.

Learning to change our lifelong habitual thinking is broadly similar to a challenge and fear most of us successfully endured as children: learning to ride our bikes. We will try to watch what we think and will fall down. At first, our negative thoughts switch-away techniques may not work, and we will fall down. Our feelings will tell us that a thought will not make us feel good, but we will not be able to stop it and we will fall down. We won't be able to stop the flow and accumulation of negative feelings, and despite our best intentions and effort, we will fall into a low mood.

Over time and with practice, we will gain the same enjoyment and sense of freedom we had as kids riding our bikes. Thinkiatry's first three principles and their one-two-three process will allow us to virtually eliminate the negative thoughts and emotions we have lived with for so many years. And, just like riding a bike, you will never forget the process.

In summary, these first three Thinkiatry principles teach us how to have a healthy psychological relationship with ourselves and manage our own thinking. Our next principle and challenge is to learn how our relationships with others and their habitual negative thoughts can also be the root of our own emotional distress. How do we deal with others who have no knowledge of Thinkiatry's principles and still maintain our own healthy psychological functioning?

We learn principle #4: **SEPARATE REALITIES.**

Principle #4:
SEPARATE REALITIES

Others not only shouldn't see things our way,
but in fact they cannot. – John O'Brien

When I discovered, studied, and learned the principle of separate realities, I had my most profound "aha" moment. I had spent most of my life thinking that one of the keys to success was my ability to persuade others to think the way I do. When they didn't, I blamed myself and the other party. I had very few healthy relationships and low self-esteem.

What Are Separate Realities?

The principle of separate realities explains that the differences among individual habitual thought systems are just as vast as those among different cultures and religions. We wouldn't expect people of different cultures and religions to see, think, or do things as we would. The unique, individual differences in our habitual thought systems prohibit this as well. It's not a matter of simply tolerating our differences in thinking and behavior, but of understanding that it literally can't be any other way.

There are no exceptions to this rule. Each of our thought systems is totally unique to itself, just like our fingerprints. It is comprised of input from our life experiences, parents, family, environment, education, work, and countless other factors that all play roles in determining our individual habitual thought system. The combinations are endless and impossible to duplicate between individuals.

Separate realities teach us that we must expect to think and see things differently than others. When we learn to take it as a given that others will do things differently, and when we understand that others will react differently than we do to the same stimulus, the compassion we have for ourselves and others rises dramatically. Understanding the separate realities principle can virtually eliminate quarrels and hard feelings.

The moment we expect otherwise, the potential for conflict emerges. This reality is true between any two people in a relationship, or internationally among nations and religions. Today, we can see examples of this principle in conflicts throughout the world.

The Futility of Trying to Change Others

This was the core of my "aha" moment described in this chapter's opening paragraph.

Our problems in relationships come about in two basic ways. We either think that others actually do see things as we do, or, as in my personal experience, we believe that others should see things the way we do because we see reality as the way it really is. As we understand and use the separate realities principle, we free ourselves from these relationship-damaging thoughts and perspectives. Others not only shouldn't see things our way, but in fact they cannot.

Our habitual thought systems make it impossible for us to see anything precisely the way another does, or for others to see things precisely as we do.

When you understand the fact of separate realities, there is rarely any reason to take what others say and do personally. Some people spend their lifetimes proving to themselves, and anyone else who will listen, that their version of life is valid, realistic, and correct. The self-validating features of our habitual thought systems will find endless examples to prove themselves right. When we understand separate realities, we begin to see the futility in trying to change someone else, or even in disagreeing and arguing with them.

As I was shocked to finally learn, there's simply no way to avoid separate realities, and if we do not accept and understand this principle, we will be frustrated and could cause more serious emotional distress. With understanding and acceptance, this principle can be a source of wisdom, joy, and humor in many of our relationships.

My Separate Reality

For years, I believed that the way I saw life represented the only and indisputable reality. I learned that I can continue to maintain any belief or opinion I wish, but I now expect others to disagree, and I can actually enjoy listening to their unique separate reality.

My understanding of separate realities has brought me closer to those I know and love. Now that I truly understand that my ideas and opinions come from my habitual thoughts and do not necessarily represent reality, other people are more open and drawn to me. I no longer approach others in an attempt to change their beliefs, but with genuine interest in and respect for their view of life; defenses drop and hearts open. I now have more fulfilling relationships than I ever thought possible. I now have relationships with others whom I had believed I could never like. I am no longer frustrated and angered by individual differences and now see others in a new light, see innocence not only in them, but in myself. I now approach others with understanding, opening the door for mutual growth.

For years, having no knowledge of separate realities and the three preceding Thinkiatry principles, I was, like most of us, constantly conflicted and frustrated dealing with my life relationships. I learned that no matter how easily I could see something, or how true a situation appeared to me, others would see things differently and be just as certain of their beliefs.

The First Four Principles: A Brief Summary

In a theoretically perfect world, the first four principles would have taught us how to create a relationship with our thinking, feelings, and moods, and we would have learned how to eliminate, manage, and control the habitual negative thoughts that have dominated our emotions throughout most of our lives.

The absence of most or all of our habitual negative

thinking represents a significant change in our daily lives. Contrary to some popular beliefs, our true happiness is not found by trying to overcome our negative thinking by creating magical positive thinking. On the contrary, we have learned that our happiness does indeed lie hidden beneath our lifetime of habitual negative thoughts.

In summary, thus far the first four principles have taught us how to watch what we think, to use our feelings as a navigational guide to let us know when our negative thoughts are allowing us to drift off course and head toward a low mood, and to understand separate realities to better facilitate relationships with others.

These four principles have created an unprecedented process and opportunity, for the first time in most people's lives, to live our lives experiencing the highest spiritual goal identified, written about, and discussed for ages, Thinkiatry's final principle, #5, **THE PRESENT MOMENT.**

Principle #5:
THE PRESENT MOMENT

The only way to experience lasting contentment and happiness is to learn to live our lives in the present moment.
– John O'Brien

Much has been written and said about "living in the moment." Spiritual teachers throughout history have suggested this advice for living a happier and more content life. However, very few of us have learned how to make this critical principle a part of our daily lives. There are a number of reasons, as demonstrated by the following questions: What is living in the moment? How do I achieve this critical spiritual goal? How does anyone move from daily emotional distress to living in the moment, and is it even psychologically possible? Once achieved, how do I make this valuable achievement a part of my life each day? Perhaps for the first time, Thinkiatry provides the self-therapy principles, process, path and opportunity for all of us to live in the moment any time we choose.

What Is Living in the Moment?

Living in the moment is experiencing life without emotional distress, clearing our minds to experience peace and happiness whenever and wherever we choose. To truly enjoy being who we are, and where we are, with no hidden agendas, worries, or negative thoughts. Time to experience, observe, and enjoy the people and nature's wonders we have always been oblivious to while living within the confines of our habitual negative thinking.

How do we achieve this critical spiritual goal? How does anyone move from daily emotional distress to living in the moment, and is it even psychologically possible? Thinkiatry provides the knowledge and skills; it's up to each one of us to provide the desire, motivation, commitment, and discipline to make it happen.

Living in the moment requires healthy psychological functioning, which may only be achieved by the elimination of our habitual negative thoughts, feelings, and moods. And we must understand the principle of separate realities to prohibit the many negative emotions that may be caused by our interactions with others. In other words, we must become proficient with Thinkiatry's first four principles to accomplish the fifth and most satisfying spiritual goal.

My Life in the Moment Experience

To be a consistently happy person, a **Thinkiatrist**, is really quite simple after the principles become an integral part of your life. I'll use my own experience to explain. Regardless of what happened to me this morning, last week, or last year, or what may happen tonight, tomorrow, or next year, I have learned that now, this moment, is where my happiness lies.

I know and understand that my life is really nothing more than a series of present moments to experience, one after another. I understand and appreciate the past for what it has taught me about the importance of living in the now. However, the past is merely the wake behind my life's boat. I see that the future is not to be feared, or a source of endless worry, but is many more present moments to experience and enjoy regardless of my circumstances. Most importantly, Thinkiatry's principles have taught me that right now, as I write for you, this very moment, is where my life is truly lived.

When I focus my attention on this moment, instead of on moments that are over or yet to be, I maximize my productivity, creativity, and ability to accomplish my goals.

As the principles become a part of you, mastering this principle becomes relatively easy. Like any other skills we learn in life, it just takes commitment and practice. Start "watching" where your thoughts are focused. I ask myself, am I totally focused on what I'm doing right now, or have my thoughts drifted towards the past or are they anticipating the future? Initially, I caught myself drifting away often, but over time this has significantly diminished. You will find, as I have, that when you are living in the moment, you'll feel happiness and contentment at a frequency you would have never imagined possible.

Let's review Part One and what we have discovered about Thinkiatry's five principles before we turn in Part Two to a discussion of how to apply them to a number of life's emotional challenges that we face each day.

THINAKIATRY'S PRINCIPLES: REVIEW

Introduction

- "Our thinking determines the emotional quality and the resulting course of our lives each moment of each day we are alive."

- Throughout our lives, we have all created our own unique habitual thought system. Today, based on the high levels of emotional distress so obvious in our personal lives, society, politics, government, religion, and so on, our book cover poses the question, *how emotionally damaged are we?* And, more importantly, the logical follow-up question is "what can we do about it?"

- The root of Thinkiatry's hypothesis and solution is that our mentally and physically harmful emotions cannot exist without our habitual negative thinking. We can't be depressed without depressing thoughts, etc. But how do we eliminate most or all of our negative thinking? We learn Thinkiatry's principles and process.

- To begin with, most of us have never thought about having a relationship with our thinking. Frankly, we have never had a reason to. But if the future of our emotional well-being and happiness depends upon creating this relationship, most of us are smart enough to know that we must.

- Learning Thinkiatry's Principles and Process will teach you that simplicity is genius. The only thing standing between us and living a healthier, happier, more content, more prosperous life is the way we have learned to think and the total control our habitual thought systems have over our emotional lives.

Principle # 1: Thinking

- Understanding the principle of thought and how we think is the foundation for healthier psychological functioning and a happier life each day.

- The first principle, thinking, teaches us that to eliminate our negative emotions we must remove or create a process to switch away our negative thoughts. In doing so, we are removing our ability to ever feel the emotional and physical consequences of our habitual negative thinking.

- Negative thoughts serve no healthy purpose in our lives. If we eliminate negative thoughts, we eliminate stress, depression, anxiety, jealousy, and so on. Emotional distress cannot exist without our habitual negative thoughts.

- The normalcy bias has protected and enabled our negative habitual thinking and resultant emotional consequences for centuries.

- Our relationship to our thinking begins with watching what we think. We are watching for any thoughts that aren't going to make us feel good and choosing to switch them away to our mental trash bin.

Principle #2: Feelings

- Thinkiatry's second principle, feelings, provides us with a foolproof guidance system to continually navigate our emotional path to a happier, more content life each day.

- When we think, we immediately feel the effects of our thoughts. The amount of time it takes us to feel the effects of a thought is the same amount of time it takes to see light when we flip the switch; most of us aren't even aware that it's happening.

- The only value in habitual negative feelings is to let us know that we are seeing life in a distorted, dysfunctional manner.

- Using Thinkiatry's principles and process we are instantly alerted to any thought(s) creating a bad feeling. At this moment, we have to choose to switch the negative thinking away or allow ourselves to become a victim of our self-created habitual negative thoughts and ensuing emotions.

- Once we understand Thinkiatry's principles and their ability to lead us to healthy psychological functioning, we are no longer tempted to analyze or think our way to happiness. Happiness is already with us and always has been, buried beneath our habitual negative thinking.

Principle #3: Moods

- When we are in a high or good mood, Thinkiatry's thinking and feelings principles and processes are doing their job. We are successfully switching away any habitual negative thoughts we may think or feel and are joyfully experiencing our own unique healthy psychological functioning.

- Conversely, in our low moods we have momentarily lost our constant battle with our habitual negative thoughts. For any number of personal reasons, usually because we have started to blame our life circumstances rather than our habitual negative thinking, we have regressed, and our negative thoughts and feelings are in charge.

- In low moods, just about everything in life looks very serious and difficult. We lose our perspective; we feel that others are out to get us, or they don't care about our problems and emotional distress— the problems and emotions that we have created with our now unchecked habitual negative thoughts. Life seems to be all about us. We take things personally and often negatively misinterpret those around us.

- Many serious relationship problems turn out to be nothing more than two people who have made a habit of taking each other's low moods too seriously.

- Don't try to solve your problems in a low mood. Your emotions in a low mood will have you convinced that your negative thoughts and feelings are real; they are bad mood feelings and are not your true feelings. The problem(s) will still be there after your low mood has subsided. After your healthy psychological functioning has returned, you will have access to your problem-solving healthy thoughts and wisdom.

Principle #4: Separate Realities

- The principle of separate realities explains that the differences among individual habitual thought systems are just as vast as those among different cultures and religions.
- When we learn to take it as a given that others will do things differently, and when we understand that others will react differently than we do to the same stimulus, the compassion we have for ourselves and others rises dramatically.
- The moment we expect otherwise, the potential for conflict exists. This reality is true between any two people in a relationship, or internationally among nations and religions.
- Our problems in relationships come about in two basic ways. We either think that others actually do see things as we do, or, as in my personal experience, we believe that others should see things the way we do because we see reality as the way it really is.

- There's simply no way to avoid separate realities, and if we do not accept and understand this principle, we will be frustrated and could cause more serious emotional distress. With understanding and acceptance, this principle can be a source of wisdom, joy, and humor in many of our relationships.

Principle #5: The Present Moment

- The only way to experience lasting contentment and happiness is to learn to live our lives in the present moment.
- Living in the moment is experiencing life without emotional distress, clearing our minds to experience peace and happiness whenever and wherever we choose.
- Living in the moment requires healthy psychological functioning, which may only be achieved by the elimination of our habitual negative thoughts, feelings, and moods.
- Regardless of what happened to me this morning, last week, or last year, or what may happen tonight, tomorrow, or next year, I have learned that now, this moment, is where my happiness lies.
- You will find, as I have, that when you are living in the moment, you will feel happiness and

contentment at a frequency you would have never imagined possible.

Thinkiatry's Goal

The goal of Thinkiatry's five principles and process is to provide virtually foolproof steps that lead to more happiness and contentment in our lives each day. Learning the steps can help ensure your own healthy psychological functioning as you apply them to your unique, ever-changing life circumstances.

No principles or plans, of any kind, have any significant value unless they can be applied and performed to accomplish a goal. In Part Two, Applying Thinkiatry's Principles, we will identify and discuss a number of the common emotional consequences most of us live with each day and how the principles are used to change the emotional landscape of our lives. Become a Thinkiatrist, and join the happiest people on earth.

Part Two:
APPLYING THINKIATRY'S PRINCIPLES

❖⟶⊃ ⊂⟵❖

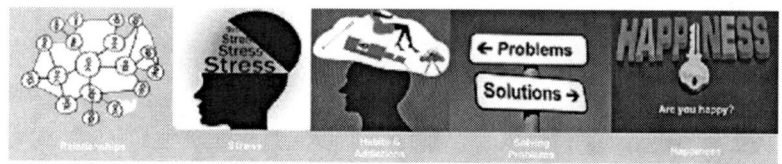

INTRODUCTION

Principles are great. They sound good and are usually created and designed to state a fundamental truth upon which other principles are based. However, as I previously explained, principles have no value unless they can be applied to a process to consistently accomplish a goal.

Thinkiatry's principles have been created to assist all of us in achieving healthier psychological functioning and happiness in our lives. Without question, this is an admirable goal for countless people. However, the principles, consisting of thinking, feelings, moods, separate realities, and living in the moment, are of no value unless we can see the value of using them each day to eliminate emotional distress in our lives. In Part Two, we will identify and discuss how the principles may be applied to a number of common, unhealthy emotional conditions most of us experience frequently, in some cases every day.

The goal of Thinkiatry's principles is to eliminate the preponderance of negative thinking that dominates so many people's emotional health in today's society.

How Times Have Changed

I have often thought about and speculated on why these principles, the first four of which were first published in 1987, were not identified centuries ago. I have discovered no definitive answer, but if asked, I would respond with the following answer: timing, technology, and information overload due to today's instant worldwide communication. As a result, our average propensity to fall victim to negative thinking has increased dramatically over the past several years, as have the damaging emotions resulting from the habitual way we think.

The 1950s were probably the last decade in which the predominance of emotional distress was pretty much confined to the immediate family, work, and an occasional violation of party-line telephone rules. (Younger readers will have to ask their grandparents about party lines and televisions without remote control; as hard as it is to imagine, we actually had to get up to change the channel.) Television and the media were very tame, and Ozzie and Harriet were most American families' role models. How things have changed!

The 1960s were probably our society's emotional tipping point. Most notably, on November 22, 1963, at 12:30 pm central time, we all suffered an unprecedented emotional shock: the young and dynamic leader of the free world, John F. Kennedy, was assassinated. We all lost some of the American dream that day, and most would probably agree that our lives and culture have never really been the same since.

Then the Vietnam War brought social unrest and emotions to the streets. Television and communication technology vividly revealed human pain, suffering, atrocities, and death. Millions were visually exposed to war in their living rooms each night. The emotional pain and fear that thousands began to experience created a growing drug culture, with people using drugs as self-treatment to feel better and to escape their own emotionally ravaged realities. The age of intensifying emotional distress began to explode throughout the U.S. and other parts of the world. Negative thinking and the resulting emotions began to grow exponentially.

Applying Thinkiatry's Principles Today

Today, more than 40 years later, emotional pain and negative thinking are epidemic. Lifetime employment and a financially secure retirement may never return. The American dream of owning a home has been decimated; our government and political system have enraged millions of people; divorce has all but erased the traditional family unit; our education system is nowhere near the best in the world anymore; and many people are beginning to believe that our capitalist system itself may be on the verge of the end of days. Some are even questioning how much freedom really exists anymore.

Individual emotional distress has reached historic levels. Millions are trying to cope with their emotions while the traditional foundations for their emotional security and happiness are rapidly fading into history. Our economy, home ownership, the family unit, and future employment are now at risk like never before. Further, problems with our medical care and social security systems are sources of constant worry and fear for millions.

Today's media, corporations, and a growing number of politicians are no longer trusted to tell the truth or act on the behalf of the average citizen. Many suspect that our lives are virtually controlled by those with billions of dollars, with corporate and Wall Street schemers paying for political control of our country. Fewer and fewer citizens believe anything they see or hear anymore.

Our political system is operated and funded by the same sources that enslave the media with billions of advertising dollars. No common man, like honest Abe Lincoln, has a chance to become an elected official today without the backing of millions in contributions to create endless slanderous and embarrassing finger-pointing campaigns with little or no substance. Who is being held accountable for what they are going to do to solve the myriad problems facing millions of Americans today? Does the average American have any representation they can trust anymore?

And it gets even worse; most countries throughout the world are in the same boat, some a lot worse. Our country's levels of negative thinking and emotional distress are growing at alarming rates. But as we have witnessed and learned over the past decade, the end result for unchecked negative thought and emotional distress is far worse. We now call it terrorism—a word and harsh reality virtually unknown to the average American four decades ago.

I am sorry to have exposed you to the previous paragraphs and the negative thoughts and emotions you may be feeling at this moment. But the truth is we must either talk about and expose these harsh realities or continue doing the same thing we have always done and expect different results, which is Einstein's definition of insanity.

There Is Hope, for All of Us

There is hope, as evidenced by another very prophetic quote from Dr. Einstein: "No solution to any problem may be found by using the same level of *thinking* that created the problem in the first place." No doubt, Dr. Einstein would endorse Thinkiatry's principles and process as a solid step in the right direction! I only wish I could transmit Thinkiatry's principles as a serum for millions to inject, rather than distributing one book at a time.

Back to living in the moment. Let's begin discussing and learning how we can use Thinkiatry's principles to help eliminate some of the more common emotional challenges we face each day. Remember, it's not our circumstances that cause the emotional distress in our lives, but the way we *think*. Let's begin with one of the most prevalent, depression.

Applying the Principles:
DEPRESSION

We largely constructed our depression. It wasn't given to us. Therefore, we can deconstruct it. **– Albert Ellis**

All of us suffer from depression at some time in our lives. After all, the only absolute certainty in our lives is our ultimate demise. When you think about it, this fact alone is negative and can cause depression if we continue to think about our ultimate fate. Further, the occasional thought of death is a perfect example of how Thinkiatry's principles and process work.

We all think about death at some frequency. The

thought instantly creates a bad *feeling* which we usually just "switch away" with another more pleasant thought. If we don't, and choose to continue thinking and creating feelings about death, our negative feelings will continue to accumulate, creating a full-blown "thought attack," and quickly descending into a low mood or even depression if negative thoughts about death become chronic. We have all used Thinkiatry's first three principles many times in our lives and had no idea that we were.

Statistics: How Many Are Afflicted?

How many of us suffer from depression? Well, if we just use U.S. statistics, ignoring the rest of the world's population, the National Library of Medicine's 2004 Medline Plus study showed that over 17 million people had experienced at least one major depressive episode *during the last year*. That's one year! The same source estimates 10–15% of women experience postpartum depression after giving birth. Depression is even more common in those with a coexisting illness, such as diabetes, cancer, or stroke. For example, 40–65% of patients who have experienced a heart attack also fall victim to their negative thoughts and develop further complications with depression.

The National Institutes of Health provides a long list of mental health statistics for Americans, some of which are eye-popping. "An estimated 26.2 percent of Americans ages 18 and older—about one in four adults—suffer from a diagnosable mental disorder.

These statistics only include those who have sought and received professional medical assistance and diagnosis. It's probably not unrealistic to assume that the undiagnosed suffers nearly double the above statistics and most certainly include some of our own family members, friends, coworkers, and others we deal with every day.

Webster's Dictionary defines depression as "depressing or being depressed; a hollow or low place; low spirits; dejection." We all have our own personal perception and definition. Most of us are afraid to publicly admit any level of depression due to society's general view that people suffering from depression are mentally unstable, unpredictable, unreliable, or mentally ill.

As previously mentioned, all of us experience some level of depression at times in our lives: after the passing of a loved one, a job loss, and divorce to name a few. Many others live their lives in quiet desperation, fearful of disclosing their chronic, depressed feelings, assuming others will judge them negatively.

I must caution that those with serious levels of chronic depression must consult with their primary physician or an M.D. in psychology. Diagnosis and medication may be required before a client is ready to rationally pursue learning and using Thinkiatry's self-therapy principles and process.

Thinkiatry represents a new field of self-therapy principles and process to work in conjunction with, or as an alternative to, traditional psychotherapy and medications.

Depression Can't Exist Without Depressing Thoughts

Thinkiatry focuses on the absolute fact that depression cannot exist without negative thoughts. Therefore, our frequency of negative thinking determines our level of depression. Thinkiatry teaches us how to minimize negative thoughts, which have absolutely no value in our daily lives except that they let us know we are off track and headed toward emotional distress.

If negative thoughts are managed and controlled, our lives change quickly, depression and many other negative-thought-induced, and distressful emotions can no longer exist, as Thinkiatry's principles alter our typically habitual negative thinking.

Most people would agree that negative thinking about ourselves and others has reached epidemic levels in societies throughout the world today, and traditional therapies and medications are not going to reverse this trend. A large percentage of prescribed medications are not even taken because of side effects and users' belief that they don't need to depend upon medications they don't understand or see value in.

Thinkiatry's self-therapy principles and process focus on the root of depression by eliminating the chronic negative thinking—the true source of all emotional distress. The principles teach us that only we choose to make our negative thoughts real, and our feelings act as a navigational tool to instantly alert us that negative thoughts are active, before they become a low mood, thought attack, or depression.

We can learn to understand, monitor, and control the emotional landscape of our lives. Imagine how your emotional life can change using Thinkiatry's self-therapy knowledge and skills many times each day to minimize the negative-thought-created emotions in your life.

Any level of depression, with or without medical or pharmaceutical intervention, may only be reduced or cured by eliminating the chronic negative thoughts that have created it.

Our Past and Future

As I mentioned earlier in the book, my childhood, like many others, was affected by a number of very personal family events that represent the wake behind my life's boat, otherwise known as the past. Thinkiatry has taught me that the wake, our past thoughts, do have positive value in the lessons learned, but have no value and may be quite harmful if we allow past negative thoughts to be resurrected, causing emotional distress today. The same holds true for creating fearful thoughts about the future; it is impossible to predict what will happen in the next hour, day, month, or year. The only certainty is this very moment. This sentence could be my last on earth, and the future will only be determined by what I do in this moment. My habitual thoughts that create fear, anxiety, and stress about the future will only impair my ability to perform and create in this moment.

After all, the future is nothing more than the accumulation of all the moments between now and then. If we make the very best of each moment by living in the moment as often as we can, the future will automatically be the best we can make it. Thoughts that lead to speculating, worrying, or anticipating the future are self-created, not real, and senseless. We must understand and value that what we do in this moment is the only real factor affecting the future.

A Low Mood with No End

Thinkiatry recognizes that depression exists in varying

degrees of severity and frequency, but is defined as a condition created by our inability to stop our negative thinking, which has now become a chronic mood. Depression is essentially a low mood that now has no end. The circumstances or reasons are really not relative to the change process and potential cure. In fact, in many cases the reasons have been created as an assumed false reality in the victim's mind.

Depression cannot be reduced or cured unless the negative thoughts creating it are eliminated. Realistically, if you suffer from depression, the only way to combat it is to learn how to eliminate or switch away as many negative thoughts as you can each moment of each day. As previously discussed, we must start learning how to ride the negative-thought-elimination bike. We may fall down a few times, but once we learn, we will never forget how.

As an example, I have referred to my stuttering, which became the scourge of my life, mentally and emotionally, and which was uncontrollable from grade school until my early twenties, when I served as a Special Training Instructor in the military. In hindsight, I believe that the insecure and fearful thoughts I created began to control my emotions at about age seven and were the root of my stutter and other emotional distress for the better part of two decades. Without any training or therapy, I eventually learned that if I did not allow my negative thoughts about my stutter to become a "stuttering attack," the emotions that physically manifested themselves as my inability to speak began to disappear. Over the years, I have made presentations to groups as large as several hundred people. I do have some negative stuttering thoughts, but as soon as I *feel* them, I immediately switch them away with alternative happier, more confident thoughts.

In summary, if you are suffering from depression, you must begin to climb your way out of the chronic habitual negative-thinking emotional hole you have created. Simplicity is genius; the hole, depression, may only be filled by eliminating every negative thought you possibly can. Switching away one negative thought, you "watch" or *feel* after another every day. This process takes discipline and practice, but like learning how to ride that bike, will soon give you unmatched joy and freedom. Is living without depression greater than the price? Thinkiatry provides the self-help principles, knowledge, and skills, but the decision and commitment to change are totally up to you.

The next most common human condition requiring the application of the knowledge and skills of Thinkiatry's principles is obesity.

Applying the Principles:
OBESITY

*Contrary to popular belief, victims of obesity don't just
eat their way to their condition, they think their way!*
– John O'Brien

A viable treatment solution for obesity cannot be discov-
ered by extreme dieting for people who eat to self-treat
their emotional pain or by insisting on the performance of
unrealistic and rigorous exercise programs for people who
are typically chronically inactive. Where's our common
sense? Nor will surgically reducing their stomachs to the
size of a coffee cup lead to a definitive solution. Don't get
me wrong; I believe all of the preceding remedies can be
marginally effective in treating obesity symptoms, but they
are ignoring the root of the affliction and the long-term

solution. The root of obesity, like our life unhappiness, depression, and other emotional distress, lies hidden beneath the way we habitually think.

Treatment: A New Focus and Method

Thinkiatry's principles and process provide an entirely new focus and method, treating obesity as a habitual negative-thinking-created emotional process that manifests itself as a virtually uncontrollable, relentless thought of food, used to self-treat emotional pain. Victims use the consumption of food to treat their emotional pain in a desperate attempt to feel better. Chronic eating to excess is an emotional disorder, a mental illness caused by habitual negative thinking, which manifests itself as an eating disorder. The cause parallels depression, in which our habitual negative thinking is the root of the disorder. But unlike depression, whose condition manifests itself in *moods* and sometimes dark emotional behavior, obesity manifests itself in the obvious form of far beyond normal physical height-to-weight ratios.

Our society has historically held (with habitual negative thinking, of course) the general opinion that those who suffer from excess weight are so lazy that all they do is lay around and eat. As a result, the programs the non-obese "experts" have devised to treat obesity are created using their own habitual negative thinking and false assumptions in an attempt to help; in most cases their intentions are sincere, although some only see an opportunity to make money—billions each year—selling their purported weight loss treatments and cures.

Adult Obesity Statistics

The viability of today's obesity treatments to help the victims may be measured by the statistics on the actual results.

Recent statistics are not encouraging. According to October 2010 figures from the Centers for Disease Control and Prevention, 2.4 million more Americans became obese between 2007 and 2009. Approximately 26.7 percent of the adult U.S. population, or 72.5 million people, are now obese. Add the overweight, but not yet obese, and almost 50 percent of Americans are overweight, equaling a grand total of over 140 million people.

Experts at the American Institute for Cancer Research (AICR) said that this increase may well result in a corresponding increase in the national cancer rate in years to come. The AICR experts pointed out that those 72.5 million obese Americans face an increased risk for colorectal cancer, postmenopausal breast cancer, kidney cancer, esophageal cancer, endometrial cancer, pancreatic cancer, and gallbladder cancer, to name a few. Annual health care treatment costs are now estimated to exceed $150 billion dollars.

Childhood Obesity Statistics

It is estimated that up to 33 percent of American children and adolescents are obese today. Over the past three decades, the childhood obesity rate has more than doubled for preschool children, aged 2–5, and adolescents, aged 12–19, but has more than *tripled* for children 6–11 years old. There must be a more viable alternative treatment that can ultimately provide statistical proof of success.

Why Aren't Current Treatment Methods More Successful?

Weight loss practitioners, including many physicians, have not focused on, nor are they even aware of, Thinkiatry's principles and the way they, themselves, habitually think. Most habitually think that the treatment that works for them should work for everybody, violating Thinkiatry's separate realities principle. Their inability to understand or relate to their own habitual thinking makes it virtually impossible for these people to see that the root cause of obesity lies hidden beneath the patient's habitual negative thoughts. Today, they don't even know Thinkiatry exists.

Practitioners and doctors live in their own separate reality. They probably eat a balanced diet, exercise regularly, and usually watch their caloric intake. Their separate reality tells them that the obese patient needs to live, exercise, and eat the way they do. As a result, overweight people are told to pretty much stop eating, that they should become world-class exercise fanatics, or have their stomachs reduced to the size of a peanut. Sad, but true.

Learning Thinkiatry's principles and process will one day universally affect the performance and humanity of all professions, particularly medicine and public services. Hopefully, one day doctors will be required to learn Thinkiatry, not only to improve their own healthy psychological functioning and happiness, but to understand that their patients have their own unique separate reality, which must be understood and become an integral part of the medical diagnosis process.

Here's a clear example of a practitioner's normalcy bias from Jeff Barnes's January 1, 2011, article *Childhood Obesity/Statistics and Trends*. And I quote, "*Overweight children are much more likely to become overweight adults unless they adopt and maintain healthier patterns of eating and exercise.*" This statement is true. However, it also implies and demonstrates that the only thoughts practitioners have are that obese people can cure their condition with diet and exercise alone. Not a single thought is given to the fact that the real cause for obesity is mental and emotional—the real treatment required has not even been thought about or considered. The present treatment consensus is the victim must stop eating and exercise like a world-class athlete. Does this make any sense?

Of course not! In fact, their prescribed treatment can severely compound the victims' real thinking and emotional problems by setting them up for even more failure. The statistics strongly infer that the odds of curing obesity by severe dieting and exercise regimens are about the same as winning the lottery.

Clearly, we can begin to understand why 2.4 million, about 10 percent, more people became obese in just the past few years.

Using Thinkiatry's Principles and Process to Treat Obesity

Overweight and obese people do not just eat their way to their condition, they think their way. Like the other habits and addictions discussed in our next chapter, eating and food are the self-treatment, not the cause, of the disorder. The fundamental causes for this disorder are chronic, habitual, negative-thinking-created emotions, resulting in unhealthy psychological functioning and the inability to cope with emotionally perceived unhappy lives. They don't really want to gain more weight; they simply don't know how to be happy and content without their addiction. They consume more and more calories to give them a few minutes of feeling good; similar to a fix for a junkie.

Please note: Thinkiatry's principles and process focus on the thinking and emotional aspects of treating obesity. A primary care physician must be consulted to perform a complete physical exam and diagnosis. Several medical conditions may cause or be the result of obesity. If you have not already sought medical diagnosis and care, do so immediately.

Most obesity victims have had plenty of time to develop their own unique negative habitual thinking. They have usually been exposed to heckling, bullying, discrimination, and generally unkind treatment from others for years. They know very well how most others think about them. How do they think about themselves?

They are generally very unhappy with what they assume is their lifelong fate and would give anything to be a normal size. They have no idea how their negative thoughts about themselves and others create harmful emotions that virtually guarantee their inability to ever achieve healthy psychological functioning and happiness. However, assuming no other medical conditions prevent weight loss,

Thinkiatry's principles, process, and path will lead them to healthier psychological functioning and happiness.

If any medical reasons for their condition have been diagnosed and treated, the only obstacle they face is eliminating the habitual negative thinking and damaging emotions that have been the root cause of their addiction to food. The amount of time these thoughts have controlled their emotional lives will vary by patient, and will determine the corresponding amount of time, work, and effort Thinkiatry's principles and process will take to virtually eliminate negative thoughts from their lives each day.

The first test will be one of the most critical; I coach obesity victims using what I call the two-step approach. After explaining that our thoughts are not reality, that we create them, I simply ask, "What are the two habitual negative thoughts that make you feel the worst?" Then these two thoughts become our target for the week. We then work through each principle and process to demonstrate how to identify these two target thoughts by "watching what you think" and to see the instant impact the targeted thought has on how they feel. We practice how to use the "switch away" technique to replace a negative thought, such as "I have to eat something," with another personal happy thought. We discuss how their feelings should never be compromised by any negative thinking that must be switched away. We look at why low moods occur, and how to change their thinking to rapidly recover. We talk about the separate realities principle, why others think and act the way they do, and why another's thoughts and comments are only harmful if we allow them to be and therefore should not be taken seriously. Then we learn how the first four principles have equipped us with the knowledge and skills necessary to achieve the coveted fifth principle: living in the moment.

Usually, for the first time, the obesity victim sees and understands how their dysfunctional habitual negative thinking has been the root cause of their weight problem all along. They are now confident that Thinkiatry's principles and process have given them the priceless knowledge and skills to change the emotional and physical landscape of their lives for the better, forever.

In summary, obesity is the result of a vicious cycle of thoughts and emotions. Most victims are not aware that the habitually negative way they think about themselves and the opinions of others, their emotions, are the root cause of their illness. Their physical condition is the result of their continuous efforts to treat the way their emotions make them feel, to find some relief.

The consumption of food becomes both their escape and their addiction. Food gives them precious moments of emotional freedom and brief happiness; yet, as with all addictions, there are serious long-term consequences.

Their plight is further compounded by the fact that most of the public, the medical community, and other practitioners have their own separate realities and no knowledge of Thinkiatry's principles and hypothesis. As a result, these groups typically concur that obese people are just too lazy and eat all the time. Their separate realities are convinced that the cure for obesity should be dieting and exercise. They don't have the knowledge and skills to understand that dieting and exercise only treat the symptoms; the cure lies hidden beneath the obese victim's habitual negative thinking and emotional distress.

Next, we apply Thinkiatry's principles to other habits and addictions.

Applying the Principles:
HABITS and ADDICTIONS

The chains of habits and addictions are generally
too small to be felt until they are too strong
to be broken. – Samuel Jackson

The words habit and addiction are really interchangeable; both describe a behavior you engage in that, if you were given a choice, you would not. We'll use the word addiction rather than habit to avoid any confusion.

Where Do Our Addictions Come From?

Where do our addictions come from? What's the most effective way to eliminate them as a source of distress and premature death in our lives?

Addictions can all be traced back to only one source: our thinking. Every thought we choose to make real creates a corresponding feeling and emotion. Thus, our susceptibility to addictions is a function of how many negative thoughts and emotions we create.

Thinkiatry teaches us that healthy psychological functioning and happiness may be achieved by using the principles and process to virtually eliminate negative thoughts from our lives each day. However, today, the only people on earth who understand Thinkiatry are those who have read this book, which has not been published yet. So, with the exception of my wife, a couple family members, and close friends, nobody knows how to achieve healthy psychological functioning and happiness from within their own thinking. Therefore, everybody else on earth must find their own happiness despite their personal level of habitual negative thinking and emotional distress.

Thinkiatry teaches us that the happiness all of us need is achieved by eliminating our negative thoughts and emotions. How does the rest of the world find happiness? Millions are not able to find it within their own thinking and self-created reality; they naturally search for outside sources to help make them feel better. Some use sports, others use their work, or at least they think they do. Many focus on living their kids' lives, others find happiness buying things, and on and on. Unfortunately, millions more reach for other substances to relieve their emotional pain or the perceived stress life causes. In other words, people need to escape from their daily, self-created, emotional drama. Quite simply, they become desperate to feel better and they search for substances to alter their feelings and mood.

How Many Americans Are Addicts?

Because all addictions originate in the same manner, the specific addictions we are working with are not important. The latest statistic I could find was published in 2008. Surprisingly, I could not find statistics that combined tobacco, alcohol, and drugs. The numbers only include users who have sought some form of treatment and registered with an agency of some kind for help. Again, I believe it is realistic to assume that the number of unregistered addicts who have not sought professional help is probably about equal to those who have. Thus, the total number of addicts is about double the reported statistics.

The 2008 reports state that over 23 million Americans

are addicted to alcohol and other drugs. Substance abuse involves the repeated and excessive use of a drug or alcohol to produce pleasure or escape reality despite its destructive effects. Although legal substances such as alcohol and nicotine can be and are abused, when we talk about drug abuse, we tend to think of illegal substances such as marijuana, cocaine, and heroin, or the misuse of legal substances such as prescription drugs or fumes from household products.

What starts as so-called recreational use of substances can spill over into craving and addiction, with dismal consequences for the user's well-being, his entire family, and the community.

The line is crossed when the drugs become a necessity, when they control the user. The individual is convinced that the drug is necessary to have a feeling of well-being or even just to get through the day. Craving for the drug of choice eliminates most other thoughts, and tracking down and using the drug takes over. Nothing is more important than getting high—not work, kids, spouse, or family. Getting high becomes so important that the individual is willing to sacrifice everything, even as the problem is denied.

For many people whose drug of choice is alcohol, the path to addiction is slower and more insidious. Because alcohol is a legal drug and many people use it successfully, those who have problems with it often go unnoticed for longer periods of time. Frequently, the person who has a problem with alcohol will be able to continue drinking, because they continue to go to work, and they will argue that their ability to work proves that they don't have a problem.

Substance abusers are often the last ones to recognize their own symptoms of abuse, dependence, and addiction. Even when they know they have a problem, drug abusers often try to downplay their drug use and conceal their symptoms. But if you suspect that a friend or loved one is abusing drugs, there are a number of warning signs you can look for.

Some behavioral symptoms include the following: angry outbursts; mood swings; irritability; manic behavior; attitude change; talking incoherently or making inappropriate remarks; risky, secretive, or suspicious behavior; deterioration of physical appearance and grooming; absence from work or school or drop-off in quality of work or grades; neglect of family responsibilities; money problems; or legal problems.

Physiological signs include the following: frequent exhaustion or weakness; unexplained injuries and infections; blackouts; flashbacks; delusions; paranoia; and withdrawal symptoms such as nausea, tremors, and sweating.

One thing we know for sure—those who successfully overcome their addiction are compassionate, kind, giving, and the most decent human beings you can find. They have learned that happiness and healthy psychological functioning without addiction can only be found by altering their thinking to eliminate negative thoughts, feelings, and moods.

The Stars, the Media, and Rehab

Today, going to rehab has become the catchall phrase for addiction treatment, principally because of our media's focus on the high profile celebrities and other wealthy victims whose addictions are so far out of control that they get caught and are ultimately confronted by family, friends, or law enforcement.

Tragically, public addiction awareness has been deeply affected by the countless deaths of high profile celebrities and others whose lives have ended so abruptly due to the use of drugs and alcohol to escape their tortured habitual negative thinking realities.

These tragedies of addiction stay in the public's mind for longer than usual for a couple of key reasons. First, the individuals lost have had large groups of fans and followers to whom they had become an icon of some level; in some cases, they have almost become a psychological member of the fans' adopted, extended families. Michael Jackson is, of course, a prime example.

Second, the average fan and most other common folk, to varying degrees, live their lives vicariously through these celebrities. Most of us can't believe that these high-profile victims, who usually have more money than they can spend, beautiful homes, fleets of cars, fame, international travel, etc., can feel so bad they have to resort to addictions to tolerate their everyday lives.

The average citizen can't help but be emotionally affected. Of course they mourn the death, but I think they are even more emotionally damaged by knowing that other human beings who, on the surface, had everything in their lives to make them happy, lost their lives to addiction. For too many, knowing this psychological fact leaves them little real hope that their own dreams and happiness will come true—some part of them passes away, too.

How Do We Help Approximately 40 Million U.S. Addicts?

Note: The first step must be an appointment with a primary care physician. The way we think and our emotional health may be preempted and otherwise affected by many medical conditions that contribute to, or have resulted from, many different addictive substances. An evaluation by a doctor of psychology may also be prescribed to complete a full medical patient evaluation.

I guess the most appropriate response to the question above would be an old saying used when we are faced with any overwhelming task: "the same way we eat an elephant, one bite at a time," or, in Thinkiatry terms, one principle at a time.

For current addicts to have any hope for a cure, they must learn some alternative way to achieve healthy psychological functioning, emotional relief of their pain, and happiness in their lives each day without the use of and dependence upon outside substances. We must understand that our inherent, powerful need to search for good feeling in our lives cannot be overstated. And as long as negative thoughts and emotions continue to control our lives, the odds of recovery will remain unacceptably low.

As I have stated previously, Thinkiatry has been created as a result of my more than 30-year struggle to find emotional health and happiness in my life. Until I discovered Thinkiatry's principles, I spent most of my life feeling insecure, fearful, empty, and alone. At the darkest times, I would do almost anything it took, even something harmful to myself, to feel better for even a brief period of time, just like millions of addicts do.

Today's Treatment Dilemma

Today, given that Thinkiatry's self-treatment principles and process are unknown, what treatments are available now and how effective are they? Like obesity, very few agencies or rehab centers, which, by the way, few average Americans could afford, are focusing on the fact that the most effective cure for addictions is altering the way the victim thinks. How do they eliminate negative emotions to find the natural happiness and contentment healthy psychological functioning makes possible? Until they do, the addict's reliance upon alcohol and drugs will rarely be cured.

Unfortunately, as with obesity, practitioners and medical treatments do not offer any real tangible proof of the viability or success levels in their treatment regimens. As a result, depression, obesity, and other addictions continue to grow at alarming rates.

It's a good thing that the mother of all learning is repetition, because, once again, the only really effective treatment for addiction lies hidden beneath each victim's habitual negative thoughts and emotions; these millions of people must learn to eliminate negative thoughts and find some peace and happiness within their own psychological functioning, or they are forever doomed to reaching for emotional relief and a few moments of freedom from other outside substances—substances that may end their lives, or even more tragic, the lives of other innocents.

Addicts, like the rest of us, must learn that the only way to achieve healthy psychological functioning and happiness from within, critical for eliminating the desperate need for outside alcohol or substance relief, are Thinkiatry's principles and process. That our thoughts are not reality; that we can watch and choose which thoughts to follow and which to discard or switch away; that our feelings can tell us with absolute certainty when our thoughts are negative and must be switched; that negative thoughts create negative feelings that serve no useful purpose in our lives; that most of the emotional pain in our lives can no longer exist if we eliminate as many negative thoughts as possible from our reality each moment. That the causes of our mood swings are the accumulation of negative thoughts we have allowed to pass through. Those bad moods cannot possibly exist without negative thinking. That we each have our own separate reality and others will never interpret life and think the same way we do, but it's really OK. That winning the battle, armed with the knowledge and skills that Thinkiatry's first four principles teach, the addict, as well as the rest of, can find peace, happiness, and contentment. The real cure for addicts and the rest of humanity, is living our lives in the moment, the fifth principle.

As a summary, let's take a few moments to reflect. We have now identified and discussed the first three areas in which to apply Thinkiatry's principles—depression, obesity, and addictions. We have just begun to identify and understand the scope of how our habitual negative thinking impacts hundreds of millions of people and their relationships every day. Just imagine how our everyday lives might change if hundreds of millions of people were consistently working every day to eliminate their negative thoughts and emotions. I just can't imagine, but I hope I'm around to share the experience.

Next, let's talk about applying Thinkiatry's principles to **ANGER.**

Applying the Principles:
ANGER

Holding on to anger is like grasping a hot coal with the intent of throwing it at someone else; you are the one who gets burned. **– Buddha**

Anger is a strong emotion of displeasure caused by some type of grievance that is either real or perceived to be real. Thinkiatry's habitual negative thinking theory attributes anger to several factors, such as past experiences, behavior learned from others, genetic predispositions, and a lack of problem-solving ability. In simpler terms, anger is caused by chronic negative thoughts and emotions ("It has to be done my way"), and low frustration points ("It's my way or no way"). Anger is an emotional reaction that is perceived to have an external cause. Angry people almost always blame their reactions on some person or some event, i.e., on their circumstances, but rarely do they realize that they are angry because their negative-thinking emotions are causing an irrational perception of the world. Angry people have a certain perception and expectation of the world that they live in, their separate reality, and when that reality does not meet their expectation of it, they become angry.

Not All Anger Is Unhealthy

It is also important to understand that not all anger is unhealthy. Anger, one of our most primitive defense mechanisms, motivates us and protects us from being dominated or manipulated by others. It gives us the added strength, courage, and motivation needed to combat injustice done against us or to others that we love. However, if anger is left uncontrolled and free to take over our thinking, emotions, and physical reactions at any time, then anger becomes destructive.

Just like an addict who is under the control of a street drug, a person under the influence of anger cannot rationalize, comprehend, or make good decisions, because anger distorts logical reasoning into blind emotion. You become unable to think clearly and your emotions take control of your thinking and physical actions.

Physiologically speaking, anger triggers the fight-or-flight response in our brain, which increases our blood pressure and releases adrenaline into our bloodstream, thereby increasing our strength and pain threshold. Anger created by dysfunctional thinking makes us illogically think of only two things: attack or defend. Neither of these options facilitates healthy psychological functioning, happiness, or improved relationships.

Our internal sources of anger come from our habitual negative thinking and the resulting emotional distress that causes chronic irrational perceptions of reality.

People who attempt to reason with their emotional dysfunction misinterpret normal events and things that other people say as being directly threatening to their needs and agenda. People who use dysfunctional emotional reasoning tend to become irritated at something innocent that other people tell them because they perceive it as an attack on themselves.

All of us at some point have experienced a time when our tolerance for frustration was low. Stress-related anxiety often lowers our tolerance for frustration, and we begin to perceive normal things as threats to our well-being or, even more common and potentially dangerous, threats to our ego.

When people make demands, they see things as how their separate reality perceives they should be and not as they really are. This lowers their frustration tolerance because people who have unreasonable expectations expect others to act a certain way or for uncontrollable events to behave in a predictable manner. When these things do not go their way, then anger, frustration, and eventually depression result.

People profiling is another anger-causing type of dysfunctional thinking in which the person applies a derogatory label to someone else. Labeling someone an "idiot" or an "ego maniac," dehumanizes them and makes it easier for them to become the target of anger.

A Personal Perspective

My personal experiences with anger over the years have pretty much paralleled those described above. The only additional comment I might add is that my anger lies much closer to the emotional surface any time my habitual negative thinking and emotions have taken control of my feelings and moods. Today, I have learned to follow Thinkiatry's Golden Rule: I can't be angry without angry thoughts, period.

Additionally, I have learned that if we really think about it, who does anger really hurt—the person, subject, or event that was perceived to create it? No, probably not in the least. The people who are angry are the only emotional victims of anger. The only way to win when you start to think angry thoughts is to immediately execute Thinkiatry's Golden Rule.

Before Thinkiatry's principles and process became a part of my life each day, my overall emotional condition was constantly on my mind. Habitually negative thinking controlled virtually all of my emotions, and there were many. Anger was always at my side. My "aha" moment came when I learned that the way I thought, my thinking, was causing almost all of the emotional distress I had to deal with every day.

I began to use Thinkiatry's first three principles—thinking, feelings, and moods—to change the way I think. The results amazed me. The first day on which I was able to watch my thinking and feelings, as negative thoughts presented themselves I shifted them away, and it really worked. Creating a total absence of negative thoughts put my emotions out of business. The experience of hours, days, and weeks without negative thoughts in control were amazing. I no longer had to deal with negative emotions and their consequences. Perhaps for the first time in my life, I was able to sit and enjoy just being me. I had, after more than 30 years of struggle and pursuit, found a process and path to live my life in the moment, experiencing healthier psychological functioning and happiness for the first time. More importantly, I had learned the principles and process to live with fewer negative thoughts and the painful emotions they create every day.

Soon my threshold for anger virtually disappeared. You can't be angry without negative thoughts to start the fire. Today, when I occasionally relapse, as we all will, I remind myself that anger will only hurt me in the end. Therefore, to pursue and make angry thoughts real is totally illogical and senseless.

Our next application is a condition that usually has anger standing in the wing, ready to pounce—**STRESS.**

Applying the Principles:
STRESS

*Stress is not what happens to us. It's our response
TO what happens. And RESPONSE is something
we can choose.* **– Maureen Killoran**

Modern life is full of hassles, deadlines, frustrations,
and demands. For many people, self-induced stress is
so commonplace that it has become a way of life. Stress
isn't always bad. In small doses, it can help us perform
under pressure and motivate us to do our best. But when
you're constantly running in emergency mode, your mind,

emotions, and body pay the price.

If you frequently find yourself feeling frazzled and overwhelmed, it's time to take action to bring your nervous system back into balance. You can protect yourself by learning how to recognize the signs and symptoms of stress and taking steps to reduce its harmful effects.

What Is Stress?

Stress is a normal physical response to events that make you feel threatened or that upset your emotional balance in some way. When you sense danger—whether it's real or imagined—the body's defenses kick into high gear in a rapid, automatic process known as the fight-or-flight reaction, or the *stress response.*

The stress response is the body's way of protecting us. When working properly, it helps you stay focused, energetic, and alert. In emergency situations, stress can save your life, by giving you extra strength to defend yourself, for example, or spurring you to slam on the brakes to avoid an accident.

The stress response also helps you rise to meet challenges. Stress is what keeps you on your toes during a presentation at work, sharpens your concentration when you're attempting the game-winning free throw, or drives you to study for an exam when you'd rather be watching TV.

Unhealthy Stress

But beyond a certain point, stress stops being helpful and starts causing major damage to your health, your mood, your productivity, your relationships, and your quality of life.

The body doesn't distinguish between physical and psychological threats. When you're stressed over a busy schedule, an argument with a friend, a traffic jam, or a mountain of bills, your body reacts just as strongly as if you were facing a life-or-death situation. If you have a lot of responsibilities and worries, your emergency stress response may be "on" most of the time. The more your body's stress system is activated, the easier it is to trip and the harder it is to shut off.

Long-term exposure to stress can lead to serious health problems. Chronic stress disrupts nearly every system in your body. It can raise blood pressure, suppress the immune system, increase the risk of heart attack and stroke, contribute to infertility, and speed up the aging process. Long-term stress can even rewire the brain, leaving you more vulnerable to anxiety and depression.

Today, many people see stress as a necessary part of success, achievement, relationships, careers, and life. The word has become a catchall to describe, validate, and explain almost everything that is wrong in our lives. A very common belief is "If I weren't under so much stress, my life would be a lot better."

Eliminating Stress

Thinkiatry teaches us to understand that our psychological stress originates in our own minds, and teaches us to understand its relationship to our thinking and emotions. Using the principles, we can begin to eliminate stress, regardless of our circumstances. Chronic stress is nothing more than a socially accepted form of mental illness that Thinkiatry's principles and process can, to a great extent, eliminate.

Emotional stress is not something that happens to us, but rather something that develops from our own thinking. From the inside out, we decide what is and is not going to be stressful. The moment we think and define stress as coming from anywhere other than from within ourselves, we have set ourselves up to experience it and are too late to prevent it.

Our stressful thoughts are no more real than our non-stressful thoughts; they're still just thoughts. We cannot deal with something that, in reality, does not exist other than in our own thinking. Once we see that there is no such thing as stress, only stressful thinking, we can apply Thinkiatry's principles and process to switch away these negative thoughts to our mental trash bin. When we redefine psychological stress as just another segment of our habitual negative thinking, we now know how to stop the thoughts and prevent the emotions from controlling our lives. We can continue to enjoy healthy psychological functioning even when circumstances are a great deal less than perfect.

Writing this book is stressful if I allow my negative thoughts to take control. Will the book help others to the extent I think it can? I have spent a year of my life on this project; will it be in vain? Can we survive economically and create the marketing plan required to introduce an entirely new word and mental health concept to an unknowing and usually change-resistant society? These are just a few examples of my habitual negative thoughts that I use Thinkiatry's principles and process to switch away every day.

Eliminating as many negative thoughts and their resultant crippling emotions as possible allows me to continue to write and plan while maintaining my healthy psychological functioning and happiness. By eliminating most of the emotional distress in my life, I am free to write in the moment. After all, my future, as well as yours, is reliant upon my performance in this moment, and the next, and so on. Our best psychological performance right now, this moment, and in every future moment, cannot be achieved without eliminating the habitual negative thoughts that most of us have lived with since childhood.

Excessive stress may often be a factor in contributing to our next application of Thinkiatry's principles, **SOLVING PROBLEMS.**

Applying the Principles:
SOLVING PROBLEMS

The significant problems we face cannot be solved at the same level of thinking we were at when we created them.
– Albert Einstein

In this chapter we will discuss how to solve problems using Thinkiatry's five principles and process of healthy psychological functioning. We will also talk about how our individually unique habitual thought systems may have helped create past problems and emotions that were often totally unreal or rooted in negative thinking, and about the fact that most of us currently think the solutions to our problems come either through changing our circumstances or through an intense process of focused thinking.

Changing Circumstances and Intense Focused Thinking

Let's begin with the former. Of course, there will be times in our lives when our circumstances are less than desired. However, it is also true that the way we emotionally react and perceive these circumstances is solely based upon our current principles of thinking, feelings, and moods. How we see and interpret our circumstances at any moment will be directly related to our current level of healthy psychological functioning: the way we are currently thinking, how our current thoughts are making us feel, and the corresponding mood level we are experiencing. In a high mood, without the influence of our habitual negative thoughts, we may see our job and marriage as the two best things that ever happened to us. In a low mood, when we have allowed our negative habitual thinking to control our emotions, we might see both our marriage and job as dead ends. In these two simple examples, and countless others, our circumstances haven't changed, only our thinking, which instantly impacts our feelings and mood level.

Again, it is our thinking about our problem, not our circumstances, that creates the problem. Remember, in low moods we will always generate negative thoughts and emotions justifying the problem and the perceived circumstantial reasons the problem exists. In higher moods, healthy psychological functioning, we will interpret our circumstances in an entirely different light and will have solutions to a problem that we could not possibly have seen while our dysfunctional negative thinking controlled our low mood.

Our circumstances are always neutral. If they really caused our problems, they would always affect us in the same way, which they don't. It is the combination of our low-mood thinking, feelings, moods, and separate realities that create perceptions about our circumstances that bring life to them.

Clearly, I think the best advise is to avoid attempting to solve any serious life issues or other problems while we are unable to switch away negative thoughts, feelings, and a resultant low mood. This option of waiting for healthy psychological functioning to return makes perfect common sense, but can often be difficult to enforce. Many of us have spent most of our lives doing the opposite.

Historically, the most common problem our habitual negative thinking has caused in our closest relationships and many marriages is our tendency to want to get to the bottom of things and to solve problems when we are in our lowest moods. It's kind of like going into a fight with both hands tied behind our backs. It makes no sense to make any attempt at problem solving in a low mood when our thinking and emotions are suffering the most.

Thinkiatry's Problem-Solving Process

Thinkiatry teaches us to have patience by focusing first on returning to healthy psychological functioning by switching away the low-mood thoughts to eliminate bad feelings and lift away the low mood.

Contrary to common practice, we should only attempt to solve problems while we have the benefit of our true wisdom—only at its peak when we are properly using Thinkiatry's principles and maintaining our normal level of healthy psychological functioning and happiness. Often you will find, as I have, that the problem that seemed so real and urgent in a low mood may seem foolish and unnecessary when you return to healthy psychological functioning. You will be amazed at how long you have lived with dysfunctional habitual thinking and the unnecessary emotional damage you have unknowingly created over the years. Healthy psychological functioning comes first. Solving problems comes later. You will quickly begin to realize how effective Thinkiatry's principles can be to change your emotional life for the better, forever.

Earlier I alluded to the fact that many of us believe that solutions to our problems may only be found by intensely focused thinking. In this approach, we try to think, figure out, make sense of, and analyze our problems.

One of Dr. Einstein's broadly published quotes warns us against this intensely focused thinking approach: "Never try to solve a problem with the same level of thinking that created the problem in the first place." The nature of problems is that we are usually stuck on something or someone and we just can't see the answer. We are trying to solve the problem with the same level of thinking and emotions. However, as alluded to by Einstein, healthy solutions only occur when we see things in a new and fresh way with healthy psychological functioning. As ironic as it may seem, we need to stop thinking about a problem in order to see the wisdom in an entirely new and different solution! Wisdom becomes nothing more mystical than seeing the problem in a new, healthy, and fresh way.

Focusing on our problems is a bad habit most of have created, resulting from our lifelong habitual negative thinking. We habitually think about "what's wrong" in our lives, and our problems become the major source of our conversations with others. Our thoughts grow with the attention we give them, and the more we think about a given situation, the more real and difficult it will seem. Our problems are certainly not an exception.

My Favorite Technique

Here is a technique I have learned to help me buy time to get my thinking, feelings, and mood back up to healthy levels before attempting to solve any problem. I tell myself that I need an answer to a certain problem within a given time frame. The time frame satisfies my fear of not solving the problem and allows me to immediately stop racking my brain to force a solution; I deliberately forget about it. Amazingly and almost without fail, the answer will pop into my head while I am driving, showering, or enjoying some time in the present moment. I am usually quite happy when the answer I get is much better than what I could possibly have come up with struggling to force my way through my emotions in a low mood. Once I learned and experienced living my life with healthy psychological functioning and happiness, hanging on to any negative habitual thoughts became senseless.

Past Problems

What about our thoughts and problems as they relate to our past? As I expressed earlier, I believe our past is simply the wake behind our life's boat and has no relevance, except adding "should have," "could have," or "would have" negative-thinking conjecture to the present moment. It is important to reference the past for lessons learned and for wisdom, but the rest of the past is history, and that's where it belongs.

Nothing we experienced in our past has to emotionally immobilize us today. Whether we suffered childhood abuse, a dysfunctional family, divorce, poverty, or anything else, it does not have to keep us from enjoying the present moment. I believe it is our ability to leave the past alone, forgetting painful thoughts or switching them to the trash bin as Thinkiatry's principles teach, rather than the passage of time, that frees us from the circumstances of our past.

Once again, we are learning that we can achieve healthy psychological functioning and happiness by using Thinkiatry's principles and process many times each day to eliminate the chronic negative habitual thinking that has controlled our emotional lives for too many years.

Next, we learn how applying our principles to our **RELATIONSHIPS** with ourselves and others will change our lives.

Applying the Principles:
RELATIONSHIPS

Lots of people want to ride with you in the limo, but what you want is someone who will take the bus with you when the limo breaks down. – **Oprah Winfrey**

Every human being functions in the same way psychologically. We all think. Our thoughts instantly create feelings. The accumulations of feelings result in moods. We each live in a separate reality, totally unique to us. We all need to live more of our lives in the present moment. These five Thinkiatry principles are true of people everywhere in the world.

The Closer We Are, the Harder It Gets

The more opportunity we have to interact with another's thought system, the greater the chance of conflict.

This is why the most difficult relationships for so many people are marriages and family relationships. For unmarried people, the most difficult relationship is commonly the one with the person they are closest or most intimate with.

As a society, we all need help, and so do our relationships. Individually, our negative-thinking emotions about ourselves and life in general are at historic highs. Our national divorce rate has been a disgrace for years, family relationships are deteriorating beyond belief, and our work relationships need a lot of work.

Yet relationships are so important to our level of healthy psychological functioning and happiness each day. Thinkiatry's principles and process provide the knowledge, skills, and path to create a new level of quality relationships most of us have never felt or experienced.

Every relationship involves two minds, each with their own unique habitual thought processes, feelings, and resultant moods. In addition, each of us interprets others through our own separate reality—our own unique habitual thoughts about what's right and wrong in the world, and the people in it.

How the Principles Improve Our Relationships

Thinkiatry's principles and process bring a whole new

perspective to our relationships. I'll use myself as an example. Prior to Thinkiatry's principles becoming my daily companions, I really had no relationship with myself and had no idea how my thoughts and emotions worked. I was unhappy and depressed most of the time, but had never heard of habitual negative thinking or watching what I think. Needless to say, my relationship skills basically consisted of trying to find others who would be willing to commiserate with me.

My first step to quality, healthy relationships was creating a relationship with my own thinking. When our thought process is negative, our feelings, mood, and relationship skills are not healthy. We are not happy with ourselves. How can we possibly create or maintain a healthy relationship with someone else when we do not have a healthy relationship with our own thinking and emotions? So, the first step in the equation for creating healthy relationships started with my own healthy psychological functioning—the first three principles.

Thinkiatry's first three Principles—thinking, feelings, and moods—teach us that the only value to negative thoughts is to let us know when we are off track and headed toward emotional distress. Few relationships or marriages can survive habitual negative thoughts from either party for very long.

Thinkiatry's principles and process teach us to manage and virtually eliminate our negative thinking; others are then drawn to us. These first three principles teach us how to achieve healthy thinking and happiness. I learned how to virtually eliminate my negative thoughts. By doing so, I found that when my negative thoughts don't become reality, there are no bad feelings and emotions. Without negative thoughts, I was free to feel contentment, happiness, and peace of mind.

Now that I had achieved healthy psychological functioning, I was, for the first time in my life, mentally and emotionally prepared to be a healthy, happy, relationship partner. Next, I had to further understand that others live in their own separate realities. I had to learn and understand that others will never think or interpret their lives the same way I do; they can't, but that's OK.

Separate Realities and Relationships

The second step to healthier, happier relationships is to learn Thinkiatry's fourth principle: separate realities. This principle teaches us that no two people have identical habitual thought systems; others will never see life and other people precisely the way we do. When we understand the separate realities principle, we no longer expect or demand that others see life our way; our relationships grow to a whole new level of understanding and happiness.

The principle of separate realities has taught me that it's critical to know and understand that our partner, or anybody else we are in a relationship with, sees life through their own unique separate reality just as clearly as I think I do. For years, I had falsely assumed that if others weren't so blind or stubborn, they would see things as I do. But the principle of separate realties taught me they can't and will never be able to; in order to have consistently emotionally positive, healthy relationships, we all must learn to take this as a given.

I believe that coming to terms with the realization of separate realities within relationships is both a humbling and liberating insight. In reality, our personalized version of life and our interpretation of others are totally arbitrary. The good news is that your version of life isn't wrong. Yours is a function of your life experiences and habitual thinking and is every bit as justified as anyone else's. When we understand ourselves and others in this manner, we expect to see things differently from others; in fact, I soon learned to enjoy watching and listening to other's thoughts and their unique life perspectives.

I have learned to take myself and my personal thoughts far less seriously. As my understanding of Thinkiatry's principles and relationships has deepened, I have become less bothered by others thinking, because I no longer take their thoughts so personally or seriously. I may completely disagree with someone else, and I now understand that's how they think in their reality, and that's just fine.

Although it may feel normal, or "just the way it is," it is not natural to feel negativity, frustration, or impatience toward another. When I do, it is a red flag alerting me that I am reverting back to looking at life and other people through my habitual thought system. But, because Thinkiatry has taught that my thinking creates my moment-to-moment experience of life, I know I must immediately discontinue those old habitual thoughts taking me away from healthy psychological functioning and happiness.

Relationships in the Workplace

Unfortunately, too many of us spend more awake time with our coworkers than we do with our loved ones. Contrary to common belief, although there are exceptions to every rule or assumption, the more time we spend with another, the more likely we are to habitually think about the things we don't agree with or like about them. Focusing on the things we don't like about them directly translates into negative thoughts. Thinkiatry teaches us that if we do not challenge negative thoughts and dismiss them using our principles of thinking, feelings, and moods, we will

suffer the emotional consequences, as will our work per-
formance and personal lives.

How many of us have at least one problem relation-
ship with a coworker that we occasionally mentally and
emotionally bring home with us? How many of us "can't
stand" our boss, our employer, or our job?

In 2010, the Conference Board Research Group report-
ed that even Americans who are lucky enough to have a
job in this economy are becoming more dissatisfied with
their jobs, according to a new survey that found that 55
percent of Americans are unhappy with their employment.
That was the highest level ever recorded by the Conference
Board Research Group in more than 22 years of studying
the issue. In 2008, 51 percent of those surveyed reported
dissatisfaction with their jobs. Interesting to note, the sta-
tistics reported regarding workplace distress are about the
same as those reporting marital problems. If we used these
parallels, we could extrapolate that about half of us have
other relationship issues outside the workplace as well.

In any event, more than half of us suffer from some
degree of emotional distress at work; more than half of
us have consistent habitual negative thoughts about the
workplace. Healthy psychological functioning, in this case
finding more happiness and better relationships at work,
cannot be achieved until the majority of dysfunctional

negative habitual thoughts have been switched away to the trash bin.

Again, Thinkiatry's principles and process must begin with establishing a healthy relationship within our own thinking, feelings, and moods. We must begin to watch and eliminate the passage of our habitual negative thinking before our feelings and moods reflect the resulting negative emotions.

The first three principles guide us to healthy psychological functioning using a foolproof, three-step process to eliminate virtually all of our negative thinking. Please remember that the negative thoughts we create about our jobs create emotional distress that only hurts the thinker! And that others live in their own separate reality and don't see their job the same way you do.

Workplace Choices

Now that your healthy psychological functioning is working, eliminating habitual negative thoughts about your work environment, you have choices to determine how active, if at all, you want to be in helping others change a psychologically dysfunctional, negative-thinking work environment.

The first choice is for you to simply focus on your own healthy functioning and happiness. Use the first three principles and stop your negative work-related thinking, and emotional distress will no longer exist. Use our fourth principle to understand both yours and your coworkers separate realties. This understanding will help all of your relationships, and you will not find yourself taking the negative thinking of others too seriously.

The second choice will depend upon the circumstances of your work environment and specific relationships. Find a Thinkiatry partner, or start a study group. Help your co-workers learn Thinkiatry's principles and process. Most people know how much they need healthier psychological functioning and more happiness in their lives; a partner or study group may be exactly what they need to overcome their normalcy bias.

In the third choice, you and your partner or work group participate in Thinkiatry coaching sessions, teleconferences, and seminars that will be available at www.thinkiatry.com.

Regarding the fourth choice, unfortunately there are circumstances in which the first three choices will not work. In these cases, do not underestimate the value of your healthy psychological functioning and happiness to you, your family, and friends. Leaving your job may be a tragic option, but no job is worth compromising or sac-rificing your mental health and relationships with friends and loved ones.

At this moment in time, we can only speculate on how significant the impact of Thinkiatry's principles and process may become in the workplace. If the members of a work group are all experiencing healthy psychological functioning and happiness, how much more creative, productive, and profitable will their business become? How much will customer service improve when performed by trained Thinkiatrists? How will teaching Thinkiatry's principles and healthy psychological functioning reduce workplace turnover, probably the most underestimated of all business operating expenses? How will politics and management incompetence be affected? Or will Thinkiatry and healthy psychological functioning become a threat to the security and competence of current middle management? Only time will tell!

Today, the relationships we do have are handicapped by our lifelong habitual thinking and separate realities to some degree, and even the best relationships can rise to even more satisfying levels in each moment by learning, implementing, and sharing Thinkiatry's principles, process, and path.

For the past few years, Alice, my lovely wife of 30 years, has been the second, and maybe sometimes the first, most knowledgeable Thinkiatrist on earth. She has experienced, as have I, the profound effects learning Thinkiatry's principles have had on our lives, our relationship, and our marriage. In fact, we sometimes look back with awe at how many years our marriage was able to survive and how much we may have missed without Thinkiatry's principles as part of our lives.

Now for the perfect segue. Let's discuss Applying Thinkiatry's principles and processes to **MARRIAGE!**

Applying Thinkiatry's Principles: MARRIAGE

Solving the Marriage Puzzle – **John O'Brien**

Marriage: the union of two people for life or until death do us part. The institution of marriage has certainly been tested and in many ways redefined since my 1950s childhood. Most of us "baby boomers to be" grew up in a time when the dissolution of marriage was strictly confidential and socially taboo. I don't recall even knowing any kids from broken homes until the mid-to-late sixties.

My wife and I have both been married once, and married to each other for 30 years. Like hundreds of thousands of others, we have a blended family: two kids are mine, one is hers, and one is ours. So we are proud veterans of preparing to nest, nesting, divorce, nesting again, and now the empty nest, where Grandma and Grandpa live. More importantly, we have experienced marriage for years, both with and without Thinkiatry's principles.

Marriage is a 24/7, relationship-for-life commitment. Two people's life circumstances have brought them together. There are two totally separate and unique habitual thought systems, and two separate realities each person uses to form his or her own unique interpretation of the world. Let's discuss applying Thinkiatry's principles to the relationship called marriage.

National Marriage Debate

Before we begin, I feel that I must briefly comment on the current national debate on same-sex marriages. Personally, as a Thinkiatrist, I am unable to support one group of people imposing or legislating the way they think and feel about marriage upon another group. People should be able to choose who they love and marry without regard to their gender, race, or private sexual orientation. After all, over the past three decades, about half of heterosexual marriages have failed, leaving millions of children emotionally scared and many financially challenged, while taxpayers end up covering some or all of the costs for health, food, shelter, and education for too many heterosexual parents—particularly the countless fathers who, despite our legal system, get away with ignoring their financial responsibility for their children.

I will use she and he while discussing how Thinkiatry's principles apply to marriage; however, I do so without any intention of supporting discrimination against any same-sex group.

The Way the Two of Us Habitually Think

I believe there are fundamental differences, perhaps genetic and biological, between the way men and women think. Science and medicine are studying this subject every day throughout the world. Any comment or insight regarding these differences is not appropriate today, but perhaps the subject of future writings. Our first goal is to teach millions of others how to become Thinkiatrists, and join the happiest people on earth.

Thinkiatry's principles and process are universal and apply to all couples throughout the world, regardless of race, religion, culture, or sexual orientation. Just two human beings trying to live their 24/7 lives together as best they can. They have never heard of Thinkiatry's principles, and have no idea how the principles can totally alter the emotional landscape of their lives and marital relationship for the better, forever.

Ladies first. She is the bride, the friend, the partner, the lover, perhaps the mother; she probably works outside the home, too, to make financial ends meet. As she grew up, her own unique habitual thought system grew with her. Her habitual thought system today reflects her perceptions of all of the people, experiences, and circumstances she has been exposed to during her life. She will have some level of habitual negative thoughts causing emotional distress in her life, just like the rest of us. The immediate issue is how far from healthy psychological functioning is she? How much negative thinking does she have to eliminate to find happiness within herself?

Personal negative thinking is where Thinkiatry's principles and process always begins, because healthy psychological functioning and happiness cannot exist until the majority of habitual negative thoughts have been eliminated. The negative-thinking emotional rollercoaster must be torn down regardless of size.

The groom, partner, friend, lover, husband faces the same challenges. He, too, has a unique habitual thought system. How consumed is he by habitual negative thoughts? How big and frightening is the emotional rollercoaster he has created to ride every day? How far away is he from eliminating his habitual negative thought demons to achieve his own healthy psychological functioning and happiness?

It is a sad reality and fact that millions of couples, married or not, wake up to this tragic dilemma every morning, and today they are completely unaware that there are principles and a process to change their fate.

As I discussed in the Introduction, I suggest that husbands and wives, or partners, team up to read and work through each principle together. The synergy created by working on how to eliminate habitual negative thinking together is magical.

Applying Each Principle

As the couple proceeds, they will begin to understand the first principle: how and why they think the way they do. They will learn how to watch what they think, that their thoughts are only reality if they choose to make them real, and how to switch away any chronic negative thoughts before their feelings and emotions are affected.

They will learn how the second principle, the principle of feelings acts as their navigational tool to let them know when their thinking is turning negative and headed toward emotional distress. At this point, they still have a choice: continue making the negative thoughts reality and endure the emotional consequences, or skillfully switch away the negative thoughts to their respective mental trash bins before they become a low mood with even more emotional consequences.

When low moods happen, the best advice is to leave each other alone. As previously discussed, one of the most common mistakes made in marriages and other close relationships is our inherent tendency to try and solve our relationship problems when we are in a low mood; it's like trying to bail the water out of a sinking boat. After all, low moods are the result of us choosing to let negative habitual thoughts control our thinking, feelings, and emotions. Leave your partner alone for a while and then help coach him or her back to healthy psychological functioning when the dysfunctional habitual thinking and emotions have subsided.

Now, after a few years of living Thinkiatry, my wife and I rarely experience low moods. We have become very proficient at using the thinking and feeling principles to virtually eliminate negative thoughts before they ever accumulate enough to become thought attacks or a low mood. With a little teamwork, commitment, practice, and love for one another, countless other couples will achieve the same, or better, results.

Please note that Thinkiatry's first three principles,

thinking, feelings, and moods, are designed to identify and neutralize each individual's level of habitual negative thoughts that create the vast majority of the emotional distress in our lives. Mastering these first three principles is critical; lifelong negative thoughts must be eliminated to insure that each individual's healthy psychological functioning is achieved. Healthy psychological functioning is simply learning how to live without habitual negative thinking and the resultant emotionally crippling consequences. Only as negative thoughts disappear each day can happiness and contentment see the light and grow.

The first three principles help each of us establish a new lifelong relationship and understanding of how our thinking, feelings, and moods work. For the first time in our lives, we know how to alter, manage, and control years of habitual negative thoughts. Perhaps as important, we now understand how our partners' thinking, feelings, and moods work as well. Once again, when both partners have gained the knowledge and skills the first three principles teach to achieve healthy psychological functioning, the foundation for their marriage enters an entirely new and exciting realm of happiness and contentment.

Now armed with the first three principles, the fourth principle, separate realities, adds a thick layer of frosting to the couples' now healthy-psychological-functioning cake. Separate realities teach the partners that they will never think and perceive life experiences in the same way. Their habitual thoughts and feelings will never be identical; it's just not possible.

About the Two of Us

As Alice and I began to work together on the separate realities principle, I, in particular, was blown away, because I, more so than my wife, had habitually thought that one of the keys to success in life was my ability to get others to see my thinking as reality. Of course, after years of self-blame and frustration with my relationships, separate realities was truly an "aha" moment for me, both personally and professionally.

For many years, my habitual thinking process told me that if only I could get my wife to understand how I think and feel, she would better understand me, and the quality of our marital relationship would grow. I, like many of us, had spent years trying to prove to myself that my personal vision of life was valid, realistic, and correct. Even worse, I generally felt the same way about all the relationships in my life. Imagine my reactions when I began to really understand Thinkiatry's fourth, separate realities, principle.

The principle of separate realities says that the differences among individuals are every bit as vast as those among different cultures. I learned that just as we wouldn't expect people of different cultures to see or do things as we would, the individual differences in our own unique habitual thought systems prohibit this as well. It's not just a matter of tolerating differences in another's behavior, but of understanding that it can't be any other way.

I was stunned and relieved. Stunned because I could now clearly see and understand that my wife's habitual thought system will never allow her to see life exactly as I do. Relieved because I no longer had to live my life with constant self-imposed pressure and the grossly false assumption that my personal success and self-worth were tied to convincing others to see life the way I do. My relationships with my wife and others were literally reborn; because I finally understood that not understanding separate realities had resulted in years of constant relationship frustration and conflict. The solution for all of us is to gain an adequate understanding of this principle and to have the humility to admit that our habitual thinking is not ever going to match another's. No matter how easily I see something, or how obviously true a situation appears to me, my wife or anyone else will assess it differently and be just as certain of their habitual thinking.

Understanding and using the thinking, feelings, moods, and separate realities principles each day will enable countless life partners to find understanding and strength in their union they never thought possible.

Over time, Thinkiatry will reduce the rate of divorce, broken families, and lifelong emotional scars, while rewarding all participants with the unprecedented opportunity to live their lives, happy and content in the present moment wherever and whenever they choose to do so.

Parenting

In hindsight, I believe that my habitual negative thinking emotional distress began to cause real personality and behavioral problems when I was about seven years old. My parents had no idea how serious my emotional problems were and would not have known how to deal with them if they had. Parents today, 55 years later, still have no idea how serious childhood dysfunctional habitual thinking and emotional distress can cause life-altering emotional scars and suffering. Our kids need to learn Thinkiatry's principles as early in their lives as possible.

I have spent over 30 years studying how our minds and emotions work. During these years, I found myself constantly reflecting upon how the knowledge and skills I was learning could have benefited me as a child.

I grew up in the '50s and '60s—a much simpler time. Yet in hindsight, I suffered from dysfunctional thinking, anger, moods, low self-esteem, and I stuttered—to the joy of my young peers. We have all heard, or personally experienced, the stories of child bullies and cruelty. I experienced it all.

I recall becoming emotionally distressed at about age seven. Although the specific details have faded, the emotional consequences manifested themselves in my inability to speak normally, even though I had no physical or medical abnormalities. For almost 20 years, I faced each day terrified that I would be called on to read aloud or answer a question in front of my teacher, peers, or friends during play time. I am certain today that my dysfunctional negative thinking about myself, even at age seven, was the root of my stammer and stutter.

Young people today, like their parents, are faced with challenges to their thought systems and emotions unprecedented in our lifetimes. Their untrained minds and fragile emotions make them easy targets for negative thinking, insecurity, fear, anxiety, depression, and countless other emotional challenges.

I am asking courageous parents to take a leap of faith, to be pioneers, learn to become a Thinkiatrist and teach your children and young adults how their minds and emotions work; the alternative to the way they currently think, why their thinking directly affects their feelings, moods, and relationships; that no two people think alike; why bullies think and act the way they do; and much more.

Thinkiatry is not a household name yet, but I could not, in good conscience, wait any longer to let parents know about the knowledge and skills they can learn to teach and improve their children's emotional lives—God knows we all need help.

Unfortunately, I can only reflect; but you can teach and coach your children and young adults in real time each day. You, like my parents, may have no idea what's really going on within your child's mind and emotions. You may be amazed, even with a preschooler, how far their habitual thinking development has already progressed.

By the way, you, your child's teacher, will also learn the skills and gain the knowledge required for healthier psychological functioning and happiness—a true win/win proposition. Simply use this book as your study guide and teach the content at your child's current level of understanding—a brief lesson each day or night. When old enough to read and comprehend, buy them their own personal copy. Then spend time reading and discussing the book together on at least a weekly basis; you will be amazed at the results.

Today, I can only speculate on how different my emotional life would have been had my parents been

Thinkiatrists. Give your kids the chance to live their lives with an emotional self-help process they will use many times each day and will never forget, and that will last their lifetime.

Applying the Principles:
HAPPINESS

"It isn't what you have, or who you are, or where you are, or what you are doing that makes you happy or unhappy. It is what you think about. – **Dale Carnagie**

Happiness lies within our own thinking and our ability to eliminate habitual negative thoughts, not a set of circumstances. If you don't understand how to achieve healthy psychological functioning, however, you won't be happy, no matter how wonderful your circumstances may be. You will continue to make negative thoughts your reality, as you have throughout your life, and suffer the daily emotional consequences. In fact, we can never find happiness by searching for it, because the minute we do, we imply that it exists outside ourselves.

Thinkiatry's principles teach us that our level of healthy psychological functioning is the gateway to happiness and living our lives to the fullest in each present moment. We can stop trying to be happy and simply be happy even when our circumstances are less than perfect.

When you are conscientiously executing Thinkiatry's principles and process, happiness is right now. Your negative thinking has been diminished or eliminated, and what's left is healthy psychological functioning, happiness, and contentment. However, we must continually monitor our thinking and feelings to recognize and warn us how quickly and easily our habitual negative thinking emotions may return.

Happiness allows us to view our lives with a new perspective and creativity. Our decisions regarding our current life circumstances are more wise, productive, and timely. Healthy psychological functioning allows our wisdom and common sense to surface so we can enjoy, rather than continually struggle with, the everyday challenges living our lives inevitably create.

Not in the Past

Our past is like the wake behind the boat. Spending time creating theories as to why our past is responsible for our thinking, feelings, and emotional health today cannot make us immune to negative thoughts. Delving into our past to uncover painful memories will not bring us happiness and is the opposite direction Thinkiatry's principles are teaching us to be focused. Excessive thoughts about our past will only serve to possibly convince us that we do, in fact, have sufficient reasons to be upset and unhappy.

In reality, our past is over, a harmless memory that we carry through time in our own thinking. We can learn valuable lessons from the past, the accumulation of which becomes wisdom, but how many times have we failed when trying to think our way to happiness?

Not in the Future

The same is true regarding the future. For years, I thought I experienced happiness right after getting something I wanted. Today, I believe that the only reason I thought I was happy was not because of a desire fulfilled, but because I had, for a brief period, taken my attention off the other things I didn't have and other future events. Many of us spend our entire lives in a cycle of "I will be happy when"; when I finish school, when I get a good job, when I get married, when the kids are grown, when I retire. In the interim, our lives and the true happiness derived from healthy psychological functioning pass away each day.

Whenever we attach conditions to our happiness, we won't find it. We will use the same thinking process over and over each time an outcome is achieved. For example, I will finally find happiness when I'm married; I know I'll be happy when we have children; when the kids start school my happier life will begin, and so on. Interestingly, most of us don't even recognize this firmly established pattern or question why we aren't happy yet. Clearly, our happiness and healthy psychological functioning must come from within.

When we understand that our happiness is simply a feeling, a state of being, that may only be experienced after dysfunctional negative habitual thinking has been skillfully carved away, we can help our happiness grow and maintain itself, as long as we can keep negative thoughts at bay.

I find it very interesting that thinking does require some effort. But our happiness really requires no effort at all. In fact, the fundamental challenge is more simply letting go of emotions and unhappiness created by habitual negative thought than it is trying to be happy. Remove the negative thinking from your life and your happiness will never desert you.

When we learn and practice Thinkiatry's principles and process, we will naturally see and feel, often for the first time, the inherent beauty and peace in each moment that is happiness in our lives. Happiness is right now, not a condition of healing the past or some future circumstance. Right here, right now! The choice is yours.

Thank you very much for making the time to read my work!

Best Wishes, John.

About the AUTHOR

John L. O'Brien was born in Lafayette, Indiana, where his parents attended Purdue University, but he calls South Bend, Indiana, home.

He was an Irish kid growing up in a Jewish neighborhood within blocks of the University of Notre Dame.

He has been married for more than 29 years. He has four children and four, soon to be five, grandchildren.

John and his wife Alice enjoy their "empty nest" status, and have lived in the southwest Denver area for almost three decades.

The only thing John has ever won in his life was the number five (5) pick for the Vietnam draft lottery in 1969.

He earned his B.A., M.A., and Ph.D. in studies related to business and human resources.

John has studied human emotions and psychological functioning for more than three decades, searching for a path to achieve lasting happiness and contentment in life.

He has founded an entirely new field of study to achieve and continually refine each individual's path to healthy psychological functioning and happiness, called Thinkiatry®.

Studying Thinkiatry® to become a Thinkiatrist has the potential to help millions of people alter their emotional lives each day for the better forever.

Become a Thinkiatrist, and join the happiest people on earth!

CONTACT INFORMATION

Readers, please register your name, email, and zip code on our website home page for future announcements, coaching, online training, and seminars in a city near you.

Website: www.thinkiatry.com

Email*: drj@thinkiatry.com

Phone: 1.800.409.4979

Blog, You Tube, Facebook, Twitter:

Please click on the corresponding website homepage link.

---

*   Please email, or call to request information regarding individual and group coaching, teleconferencing, seminars, speaking requests, and book signings.

CPSIA information can be obtained at www.ICGtesting.com
Printed in the USA
BVOW03s1053100914

366266BV00033B/1059/P

normality. My siblings and I had become distrusting of the NHS and felt that the only way to ensure her care was for us to come in two at a time wash her and keep a vigil around her to make sure that she was safe and being cared for. Newham General is a short stay hospital, they were and are overrun, under budget and serving a capacity of area that is just ridiculous. Thus due to the fact that they were over run with agency nursing staff and budget cuts they did not always exercise the care needed for a caring profession. We witnessed the elderly patients being left to sit in their own urine and faeces for hours. The following year the hospital asked us to hold a family meeting with the team of doctors and nurses responsible for her care. They asked if they could withhold medication from her when she next caught pneumonia, it was as though it was expected. My siblings were then asked to allow them to commit 'medical murder', in our eyes. We told them that our mother was a devote woman of God and a Seventh Day Adventist and would never want to give sanction for that we felt that the Lord would come for her in his time. Mama's birthday is the 22/12/22 and on her 74th birthday in 1994, I was lying with her on her bed in the hospital, one of my sisters and my father were also visiting. However, they had left the room to speak to staff. Mama coughed a black substance up and said "Where is your sister", I said which one shaking her for more acknowledgement. But nothing, then my sister and my father entered the room to me flustered insisting "She spoke" but she never spoke again and as I have five other sisters I never knew which one she meant or why she wanted her. Eventually we got our mother into Samson Street Hospital, this was a Long Stay Hospital and essential to our local community. It has since suffered closure due to government cuts. However most of the staff knew Mama as the majority of the nurses were older Caribbean women who had come to England in the 1950's and 1960's and they were her childhood friends from 'back home' or when she first came to England. The minute Mama was moved to Samson Street Hospital my family felt at ease, we could finally breath a sigh of relief. A lot had transpired in my family over the years and a family that was once close-nit had just drifted apart because of all number of hurts and unforgiveness done to and against each other myself included. Without Mama to head, steer and guide the ship, it had sunk. Growing up we were always encouraged and empowered to speak our mind, it was like a democracy in our home. My siblings always had meetings for everything, it was a tradition. They invariably descended into loud shouting with heated tempers but we always calmed down in the end and came to amicable decisions with compromises based on logics, votes and facts. After four years and several conflicts and confrontations, Mama died and was finally taken but to add to our grief we were called to the last rites on three separate occasions before she passed. Mama was a real 'old school' fighter and a testament like many others to the proud Post World War Immigrants who were actually asked to come to England in the 1950's onward to rebuild this country, often without thanks or credible recognition at times even to date.

It was all too much for me. I was unhappy about the whole situation and some parts of her early care. I was carrying on and putting on a brave face but deep down inside I walked around silently screaming all day. I felt that I was about to breakdown. By this time I had met and married my now late husband Maxwell Barrington Grant AKA Ranking Trevor, he is a Reggae Artist who gained his fame in the 1970's in the Jamaican dancehall scene. He had come to England in the 1980's on tour to promote his career, with artist like: Captain Sinbad, Billy Boyo, Early B and Little John. All Jamaican DJ's which were well known in their time. He was nine years my senior, thus through the age mixed with the cultural differences life was not easy. In 1994 he was then forced to return home to live in Jamaica and leave the children and I. I found myself experiencing all sorts of emotional turmoil and bereavement, it was all too much to bear. My life now consisted of traveling back and forward to Jamaica twice a year or more if finances allowed. I was married but felt alone. The children and I had attempted to live in Jamaica for sometime to ascertain if the move would be right for us as a family allowing us to stay together. We considered the children's education and the implications of the move on their future and decided against it. We agreed that it was not the right option for our children. We decided that they needed the opportunities afforded to them and present at home in England for the best start in life possible. We then had to find another way to be together.

I went back to college and completed my GCSE's. Jim Carter was my English Lecturer. He had a striking Liverpool accent and his name reminded me of the former American President Jimmy Carter. He gave me confidence because he was always impressed with my stories and he would constantly tell me that I have a talent and gift for writing. I will never forget him. Jim kept asking me to join the Access to Higher Education Course after I completed his course. He would say you would be a great candidate for Access. I would say yes but inside I was afraid and had no intention of undertaking the course. I had no real tangible self confidence, esteem or worth within myself so I felt that he was just humoring me. He made me begin to question who I was or even that I had no idea of my own interest, goals and achievements. At the end of our final lesson he marched me round to the Access Department and after speaking to the lecturers I enrolled still petrified. I had no true sense of self.

Jim reminded me of my younger years, ambitions and dreams before I became a mother and wife. I remembered when I was five years old I was given an award in my school, Elmhurst Primary School for writing and making my very own book, it was displayed in the corridor for all to see. That is when I first realised that I had a talent for writing. Mainly because of the way that my teacher Mrs Stud was so impressed and encouraging. She even called me out in assembly and all the teachers and children clapped and said well done. There was also a time that people and peers always thought of me as a bully or just a funny but unusually 'strange child' as I would read newspapers when I was eight years old. My childhood friend Sandra would look at me bemused and ask me what I was doing and I would reply reading the newspaper, with a sarcastic and matter of fact tone and manner. I have always had a thirst for knowledge. Growing up I had always wanted to become a Journalist or an Air Hostess as I believed that it would allow me to travel all over the world and explore. I left school with no formal qualifications even though I took my mock exams and passed. I had began to truant and mix with the 'wrong' sort of friends. I then decided to spite my teachers, I would not attend the actual exams and get a certificate, I knew that I was clever, but I was young and had no idea of my stupidity as I actually only harmed myself. I had my daughter in 1985 and my son in 1989, after having the children and during I undertook many different courses from Carpentry, Car Mechanic, Plumbing, Bricklaying, Electronic and Electrics to Social Work and Office Administration, Sociology all sorts. I started to feel that all the certificates that I had were just pieces of paper and they were all worthless. I made up my mind I was not going to study anymore unless it was a degree. I passed the Access to Higher Education and went straight to University. I went to Jamaica to work out my next move with Trevor and my marriage.

It was now 1998 and I was virtually a single parent with two children. I was studying at university and in my second year. Then my friend Terri said "Why don't you try coming to my church". That was the start of my knowledge and awareness of my need for the Lord in my life. I began attending Elim Pentecostal Church in East Ham based in East London.

The shaping of my talent

Whilst at university my specialism and specific genre of writing excelled and became more refined. I had found my niche. The issues and topics that I was being introduced to in seminars and lectures provided a stimulant and supported in shaping my political, social views and opinions. The correct knowledge is most definitely the key to the power. I began to realise that unlike previously at school I now loved learning along with my new discovered passion. I had been married to a musician for years, I wrote lyrics for him and supported him in his creativity and career in every way. Not realising that it was part of what had drawn us together. The creativity and love of words that we shared. It was finally my turn to explore me.

My writing style began to take shape and become identifiable. Along with all of the newly acquired knowledge I was gaining, I was achieving A and B Plus, my predicted grades were a 1st. I flourished whilst studying at university I matured, grew, blossomed and evolved. Looking back I was young and my energy and vitality for life were unbounded. I was a very active student and always looked to resolve issues and concerns which affected large proportions of students to campaign for improvements and change. One of the issues which I found was a large number of mature adults struggled with grammar which affected their grades. Therefore they were either scrapping by with a pass mark of 40% or not achieving a pass at all. The need for support with English grammar was a real issue. In response I decided to set up a writers group for women to provide support, share knowledge and improve study skills to complete assignments. I found that they had qualified for entry to a degree course. However, they lacked the study skills and structure needed for effective study as they had been out of a learning environment and education for sometime. That meant that students lost marks on assignments for poor execution and use of grammar, spelling, punctuation and general sentence structure. I faced some opposition from male students who deemed the group to be sexist. They argued that the group was unfair as they labelled it as not exercising equal opportunities and sexual discrimination. I fought it and won as there was a need for what I was proposing and they did not actually want to join or even set up their own group. I was voted Student and Year Representative three years in a row by my follow students. I was also very active in the Student Union. I joined the Journalist Union and began to become even more politically minded and active. At the time I found the writers group becoming a lot of added work and pressure as the reality meant that I was undertaking to support all of students with their assignments proofing, editing etc as opposed to us helping each other. I definitely felt a little as though I had bit off more than I could chew. But God always knows what he is doing as I later went back to university and completed my Postgraduate Qualified Teacher Status. He prepared me without my conscious knowledge.

It was during that period 1997 when the idea of establishing a community creative writers group in my local area to raise literacy standards first dawned on me. I also decided that I would write a book one day. I began to develop views and opinions on many issues. I embraced university life, to a point as I was still a single parent mother with responsibilities of my children and family who always come first. Representing my colleagues I drove home and campaigned on several issues of concern which exacted changes to curriculum and procedures which exist today. Due to my route to study I had come fresh out of an Access to Higher Education Course in Newham College of Further Education, NCFE. I studied English, Mathematics, Literature and Media. There was also a 15,000 word Independent Study which was also part of course requirements. This turned out to be just a dissertation in disguise designed to rule out all who were not serious about higher education but liked the idea and it sure did. This course put me in good stead for higher education. The course prepared me. Thus I passed the course and enrolled in university the following year. My whole routine now changed to accommodate my study and take care of my children. I left university 3pm every day to collect my children from school and tend to them. I supervised their homework, read to them, we would play, spend family time, I fed them then bed at 8pm. I would then clean the house, prepare or sometimes cook dinner for tomorrow, have a half an hour break then 11pm study and work until 2am start again at 5am. That was my life during that period.

I did not really pray or even read the Bible frequently at home back then, mostly really at church.Then did not really visit the Bible again until the following Sunday. Oh, I felt the Lord working in my life on a regular basis. However, it was not until I began to pray regularly at an appointed time usually between 5-6am every morning to start the day as it is quiet. That would be followed with sometime in reading the Bible and study. Thus I would take notes and try to make sense of the text and Gods word. I would translate it into my everyday life and I ask for the Lord to help me to understand his word and implement it. I would ask for wisdom and understanding like

Solomon and for guidance and support to fulfill whatever purpose I had been designed for.

In Gideon the Lord appeared to Solomon in a dream by night and God said
'...Ask what I shall give thee...I have given thee an understanding heart, so that there was none like thee before thee, neither after...I have given thee both riches, and honor so that there will not be any among the kings like unto you...'
2 Kings 3:11 KJV

I began to realise as I truly made him the center of my life things and circumstances started to change and transform in my life. I would never say that having a committed prayerful routine is easy to achieve it takes years of practice and dedication, for everyone the time spent within the Lord's presence is undertaken in a personal unique way to each individual. It is a time for peacefulness, thankfulness, gratefulness, stillness, forgiveness, sorrowfulness, devotion, celebration, praise, honour, worship, rejoicing and acknowledgement of an all round adulation. It is a feeling of release and that sweet surrender that is only gained through an intimate relationship with the Lord of host our Almighty God above in Heaven who looks down from upon high and sees us all in all of our ways at all times nothing can be hidden from him. He knows all, sees all, knows your heart flaws and has authority to enter anywhere, situation, time, to use it for his purpose. He is the all powerful no one can deny him they will be exposed.

There was a time when I did and said all sorts of immoral things. Thus I found myself in many negative situations with not necessarily the most positive ways of dealing with them. For years I went to church on Sunday's. I walked in dutifully with my Bible and I referred to it as and when directed. I Prayed when instructed. In time I eventually became one of the welcome team. I set up communion, set up the chairs for service etc. I considered myself to be at least the stereotypical idea of a follower. But I still felt like an inadequate follower. Whenever the pastor leading the service called the congregation for mass prayer with each other. I would turn to pray for the sister or brother sitting next to me, mostly dreading it, feeling as though I was an incompetent prayer. Upon reflection, these thought processes imitated 'Agent Provocateurs' and they served as diversions which were one of the factors that caused me to question how good a Christian I actually was. It always seemed as though I ended up with a prophetic prayer who could pray for 10–15 minutes which felt like 30 minutes. It would then be my turn and my prayer was usually short and it only took a couple of minutes. However as I have grown in faith I am now uninhibited with a strong sense of the word and the importance of the Holy Ghost and when I now pray I allow the spirit to give me utterance, then a sense of letting go and surrender to the unexplainable there is a supernatural experience occurs.

Chapter Two

Transformation

Transformation

I was going through a transformation in my life and I felt that I was at a cross road as a parent, wife and part of my personal growth cycle. I made a decision that it was time to begin to actively give my children a spiritual grounding in God. Not as I had done up to that point which was attend our local Catholic Church for Christenings, Funeral, Weddings, Communions and Confirmations. I attended Mass because not a being a practicing Catholic meant your child could be refused entry to the local school, Saint Anthony's. Everyone knew that it was the best primary school in the area so every parent wanted in.

My search began with me only being sure of one thing, which was I needed to build a real relationship with God. I could then support my children in building their own relationship with God. I needed to consciously instill the importance of spiritual values and the need for spiritual growth within my children's lives. I saw it as my duty as a parent. I decided to commit my life to the Lord and was saved in Elim Pentecostal Church. I gave my life to the Lord alongside my two children. I will never forget it. The children and I were escorted to the back of the church with my friend Terry as the service had ended. Then late Terry Dexter one of the elders asked us if we wanted to be saved and give our lives to the Lord. We all said yes and we were asked to say the Sinners Prayer.

Sinners Prayer:

"God be merciful to me, a sinner. I repent now of all my sins and turn from them and I place my trust alone in the Lord Jesus Christ for Salvation. Make me a new creation in Christ Jesus and give me power in my life to live for Thee and serve Thee. In the name of Jesus. Amen."

Strangely, I thought that nothing was happening to me, even though upon reflection it was. I did not feel or even realise that there were in fact changes occurring within me. Thought processes were being challenged and I found that I felt comfort at church.

I would love to say that was it but that carried on for at least another five years. I did not understand what was happening or how I was changing but questioned and fellowship with other Christians I met and in my church. I consulted church leaders, because I could not understand why it was so hard to surrender from the Spirit and divert from the flesh. I heard testimonies at church but none of them seemed to apply fully to me, I could not identify. All of the testimonies were I was saved and I stopped smoking or drinking or even partying just basically, "I became deeply spiritual and 'Christ like' over night after being saved. Although I did not feel that I could relate, I carried on.

Fellowship: Terry Dexter

The late Terry Dexter was one of the Deacons at my first church. He was also a great family man. For all intense and purposes he was an effective example of an extra ordinary man who was a 'Man of God', who loved the Lord and his work for the Kingdom. Whether it was his job of gardener tending to the upkeep of the church grounds or his work in the community, he put his heart and soul right into it. He had an impact on many people's lives due to his outreach work specifically in community. He always reached out to me as I did not live in the local church area. This meant that he would have to ride his little peddle bike about three miles all the way down to my house to fellowship with me and ensure I remained included. Rain or sun he would faithfully visit me in all types of weather dutifully without complaint. We would discuss my struggles and life and many intimate and private matters as I would with a parent because my mother had passed and there was always a communication breakdown with my father through out my childhood so I felt alone. Mama was the only one who understood and accepted me for me flaws and all. Terry would guide me without judgement through reflections of examples of his own past before he was saved and his current struggles using the Bible for guidance and reference. He supported me in my first attempts to use scripture as a guide, improve upon problem solving and taught me study skills to reach scriptural resolutions independently with prayer and consultation with the Lord. He became like an older trusted, respected, confidant and friend as well as a brother and leader in Christ. He laid the foundations and teachings for me to learn how to work through worldly issues in Christ. Terry would pray with and for me and my family and he always reminded me that I am a child of God and I am not the same as before, I was transformed. I now had hope in Christ. Terry and Terri were my biggest supporters in my early walk.

Then the time came when he was diagnosed with `the big 'C', Cancer had been found in his neck. His faith never wavered, diminished, ceased or even questioned God. In fact his faith and love for God became stronger. A man of God he would travel all over the country to meet with popular faith healers to receive healing. He used a combination of recognised medical treatments with prayer. The cancer began to retreat for around six months and he was in remission so he was back in church. It seemed like it was all too personal and sensitive to enquire. However, health meant that he had to lessen his workload so our visits stopped but we maintained our fellowship on the telephone and at church because he needed to deal with his health and his family. Our fellowship was then maintained by telephone we would speak for one to two hours at a times.

Whenever I was not at church he called to check that I was alright. I remember how it affected him not carrying out his work and pastoral support speaking to people. One day whilst I was discussing an issue with him, suddenly he said "Thank you Tina", I asked what for and he said "You have taught me that I can minister and fellowship over the telephone". He realised over a long period of in depth telephone calls, he could still find comfort in carrying out his ministry by telephone.

I believe in what I call 'God encounters'. They are encounters which occur with others which serve to further your purpose. They are here to bring us to and inline with individuals that the Lord needs to either teach, care or use for preparation to bring us to our God given purpose in life. Ironically that is how I undertake a lot of my ministry and evangelism today through my writing and media communication systems. I feel that the Lord used Terry as an example for me to reflect upon and follow much later in my walk with Him and I see the fruits today. I never understood what Terry was doing then and how he was ministering to me and supporting my growth. Today now that I have grown and am stronger in my faith and spiritual understanding, I can see how good this man really was, he had a big heart and was on fire for Christ. The Lord used Terry to sow the seeds needed for much later. The cancer came back later and Terry passed in 2006 and went onto be with the Lord.

Baptism

It was 2005 Trevor and I had begun to drift apart, all number of hurts had transpired. I grew tired of traveling back and forth and I felt that he was not trying hard enough. I had grown up. I had evolved and I felt let down by Trevor. He was suffering from depression due to the stagnation of his career. Additionally, he was constantly being swindled out of money and revenue for gigs and Royalties by producers and so on. It all took its toll and he was so disenchanted he began to focus on recouping his royalties and his back catalogue of music, he had time for nothing else. He said it was his legacy and lifetimes work, it became an obsession, which later got him killed. I deal with this in the book: To Ranking Trevor with Love: Death of a Reggae legend Coming soon. He refused a separation or divorce, stating we promised to be together till death do us part, which I explore in the second part of this book. I didn't have the emotional energy or strength to fight it. Thus we stayed as close friends as he had grown distrustful of everyone except me. I had completed my first degree and was undertaking my Post Graduate Certificate in Education

PGCE in Teaching. By now my life had greatly changed. I was now working full time as an English Teacher and part time as a Youth and Community Worker for my local education authority. My daughter had enrolled in university the same university which I had attended so my life had really come full circle. My son was about to leave secondary education and enter into 6th Form college. Life was stressful with the test and trails of parenthood with teenagers and life. I did not feel ready for baptism because I had no real idea of what it truly meant.

Peter said: '...Unto them, repent, and be baptized everyone of you in the name of Jesus Christ for remission of sins and ye shall receive the gift of the Holy Ghost...'
Act: 2:38 KJV

For years my Pastor, Deacons, Terry, and my church sisters and brothers encouraged me to get baptized. I believed that I was still doing things that were not in Christ and felt that I was not worthy enough. I was now praying regularly. For a while I was not sure if I was doing it right or what I was suppose to feel after praying. I set aside a time every morning to pray and read my daily devotional 'Word For The Day' from UCB Gospel which gave me words of encouragement and wisdom before I left for work each morning. Still I was not reading and engaging with the Bible as much as I should apart from on Sunday in church. Thinking back my life was changing but still slowly at the face of a tortoise running a steady race. I never took the matter lightly. I had been discussing baptism with my pastor and I decided that I was ready as I was ever going to be. I knew that by this time that I could not undergo the transformation required alone. I was finally baptized in 2005 eight years after I after I first stepped foot in a church. That day was like walking on air and I felt a sense of release and exhilaration. I had moved to the next step and I was definitely a work in progress.

The act of baptism is like a seal through the symbolic nature of the immersion in the water, you are reborn and now you can leave it to the Lord to guide, heal and support you in what is right, if you trust in Him. You are now a work in progress. He accepts you with all of your flaws so that he can correct them to his specifications but you must want that change.

'They that are whole need not a physician, but they that are sick. I come not to call the righteous but the sinners to repentance.'
Luke 5:31-32 KJV

He will make all the changes necessary in you for the transformation in His time, just trust in the Lord. In John he looks at Nicodemus a Pharisee and ruler of Jews and his questions regarding being born again. He acknowledges that the public ministry Jesus had been carrying out must have come from the Lord. But almost sarcastically he ask how can a man be reborn.

"Jesus answered...No one can see the Kingdom of God unless they are born again.'
How can a man be born when he is old? can he enter the second time into his mothers womb, and be born?...Except a man be born of the water and of the Spirit, He can not enter into the Kingdom of God. That which is flesh is flesh and that which is born of the Spirit is Spirit... "
John 3:6 KJV

All of this transformation into living a Christ like life takes time as it is a process to unlearn habits and ideas that have taken a life time to learn. To be a follower for me has been to adapt to a new life style and way of thinking and being. It is to take responsibility for my actions and question what I could have done differently first and foremost. It is a constant battle with my flesh and my Spirit. I have to monitor my thoughts, actions and what comes out of my mouth.
The Bible says '...Death and life are in the power of the tongue...'
Proverbs 18:21 KJV

For me that means that I literally have the power to control my destiny in my mouth. If I speak positive that is what comes back to me, by the same token if I speak negatively that is want comes. It's like the laws of attraction in the universe.

Every disciples journey and times are different and can not be compared, judged or measured, unless by the Father. An individual described as a 'good person' who does good deeds and is a generally an all round decent human being is viewed by non believers as the kind of person that would definitely go to Heaven. However, according to the word in the Bible. It states that person will still not enter into the Kingdom of Heaven unless saved, baptized and reborn in the Spirit. This is not what I say it is what the word says. Although, I did not always believe it, I do now. I sceptic.

Living on purpose

Issues occurred in my church and I decided it was time to to leave. I explore what I learnt in second part of this book: The Scars and Flaws. I never questioned Gods love for me but I questioned my worthiness and I went through a dark period. I was out of church I had in effect backslid. I had not been in church for a year. I continued to pray and study my Bible at home and fellowship. Whilst questioning God about what I was going through and what lesson needed be learnt. I prayed and asked the Lord to send me to a church of his choice that is where I should be. The Bible says ask for what we need. Thus I asked for a church that was close to my home. Previously, if my car broke down I would not always want to use London Transport and get the bus so that would be an excuse for poor attendance. I began a 'church crawl' which is like a 'pub crawl' but instead of going to different pubs I went to different churches all Pentecostal mind you. When I heard of a church that was good, I would be there. I begun to read Rick Warren's book A Purpose Driven Life In 2007 but the book was given to me back in 2005. The book started by telling me that I was about to go on a 40 day journey. It even claimed that I would see a difference in my life before the end of the book as I interact with it. I would read the book memorize the selected scripture, then answer the questions to ponder. You were also directed to keep a journal. It was necessary to dedicate at least one hour a day to complete the task. The book began to take on its own life and as I read in solitude I felt the author speaking to me and the Lord working in my life. By the time I had reached 30 days I found the church the Lord sent me to. I was now a member of the ARC it was situated five minutes walk from my house.

I began to attend the ARC Church and quite quickly became a member. My Senior Pastor, Peter Nembhard and I had several meetings, and had discussed certain issues which had arisen during my walk and journey. He then suggested that I allow him to baptize me again as he said that I may not have been baptized in the Spirit. I had no idea that the reality of a second baptism was even a possibility. I was taught that you were only baptized once. I then was advised that I could be baptized again as the first baptism may not have been in the Spirit. Thus it may not have been sufficient. I prayed about it for sometime and then I agreed and was re-baptized in The ARC Church in 2007 along with my daughter whom was baptized the following week. This time I felt a sense of calm and peacefulness, it was different. It was great an ex-colleague named Charlotte which knew me previously commented that she was overjoyed and shocked that I was in her church let a lone giving my life to Christ. Everything happens for a reason and I believe that I have finally found where I need to worship and praise. Membership in The ARC has been a totally different experience as a follower. It is whilst I have been here that I have been seriously tested, undergone several trails in my life. In so doing confirmed my ministry which is to teach, write and preach the word illustrating its relevance today.

'My tongue is the pen of a ready writer...Grace is poured into thy lips...'
Psalms 45:1

A large portion of the ministry which I undertake is mainly outside of the church within the community and among my friends and non-believers. A lot of my friends are agnostics they believe in God but do not necessarily practice and I believe that it is important not to lose sight of who I was before so that I do not forget how hard it was for me to transform and evolve I always have understanding for others un-saved. The bible tells us we need to change the way we think.

'...And be not conformed to this world: But be ye transformed by the renewing of your mind, that you may prove what is that good and acceptable, and perfect will of God.'
Romans 12:2 KJV

Our pastor is a powerful, honest yet humble man of God whom demonstrates his love for his family and congregation through his works. He encourages us to harness our God given talents in every way. Our church is radical and real that is why the Lord directed me there. My church has recently experienced perilous times with diversions occurring within the ministry members. I have prayed about it and stood firm as the Lord cleansed and set a revival. The Lord knew that I needed a leader who had been through a similar journey to myself. My pastors testimony is definitely a powerful God guided story of triumph over adverse circumstances. Our church motto has now changed to 'Believe and become'.

'Thou art Peter, and upon this rock I will build my church; and the gates of hell shall not prevail against it. And I will give unto thee the keys of the kingdom of heaven:and whatsoever thou shalt bind on earth shall be bound in heaven:and whatsoever thou shalt loose on earth shall be loosed in heaven.'
Matthews 16:18-20

Blessings

Blessings

Paul writes, regarding spiritual gifts in 1st Corinthians 12 KJV, as he details and talks of the diversity of gifts available from the Father within the Kingdom to His servants.

"Now concerning spiritual gifts, brethren...But the manifestation of the Spirit is given to everyman to profit withal. One is given by the Spirit the word of wisdom: to another knowledge by the same Spirit... To another prophesy: another discerning of the Spirit... For the body is one, and hath many members, and all the members of that one body, being many, are one in body: so also is Christ. For by one Spirit we are all baptized into one body..."
1st Corinthians 12:1-13 KJV

For me this means that we are still one body as a part of the church as a variety of denominations in the Christian faith.
Translating and applying biblical scriptures for me has been a challenging aspect of my journey and continues to be. Walking in Christ for me means that I have been given the gift of the Holy Ghost in order to come in alignment with God for the purpose of having an intimate relationship with Him, my brothers and sisters in Christ and so the Kingdom of God. Here on earth and in Heaven worship, praise, honour and glory is given to the Lord and all who are working towards Gods purpose. Since coming into Christ my conscience has been made even stronger through the gift of discernment. Intern I have been able to grow closer to the Father and strengthen my spiritual walk and journey. The Spirit of discernment makes me have honesty, even when I do not wish to. Being in Christ is what differentiates a normal human conscience to the Spirit of discernment as the latter involves Christ. A conscience in Christ means that even when no-one else knows my secret I know that God knows and he knows my heart and intentions. Thus when I have done something that is incorrect my Spirit will not rest and I can not sleep or even settle. Understand me when I say can not settle. It is as though, when I have a secret the Lord reaches deep down into my soul and uncovers it.

Until I either confess it to Him or make it right, by my Spirit and in Christ my Spirit refuses to settle. The moment that I have acted in the Spirit on the situation I feel instant relief. The Spirit of discernment will not allow me to lie to God or even myself. You see I have come to realise that God really does know my heart and nothing can be hidden from him. I believe that He has placed the Spirit of discernment in me to act as my guider.

The Gift of Dreams

'...For God speaketh once, yea twice, yet man perceiveth it not. In a dream, in a vision of the night, when deep sleep falleth upon men, in slumberings upon the bed; Then he openeth the ears of men, and sealeth their instruction. That he may withdraw man from his purpose...'
Job 33:14 KJV

Joseph, Jacob, Samuel, Job, Jeremiah, Daniel and many more characters from the Bible were given dreams to do the Lord's work and purpose. One night I dreamt my mother and she said, "Read your Bible." It was so simple but profound. The concept of prophesy and the gift of dreams is something that I grew up with being from the church. Dreaming for me was so culturally commonplace that I never really thought about it as a gift, my siblings and I just knew that dreams literally sometimes came true. Mama, always had dreams, premonitions, signs, warnings, messages in the form of dreams. Growing up, Mama had the gift of dreaming and she always interpreted dreams for others. She told me that the Lord sent her dreams and her grand mother would always come in a dream and give her a warning or message for something bad which was going to happen. That would intern allow her to be forewarned and forearmed as she knew what was coming so was able to act with the Spirit in the situation. I watched my siblings having dreams themselves and thought nothing of the magnitude. Through my upbringing none of my siblings and I have ever ignored dreams but as passing of time they became agnostics and ran from the word and our parents teachings. We as a family have always been guided by dreams.

People would come for her to pray for them, but still I thought nothing of it, as a child I overlooked those things. She was described as a spiritual woman by all whom knew her. Mama never left her Bible an inch she would resort to that Bible for every piece of guidance and advice you name it her famous saying was always "Take it to the Lord in prayer and stay in the word." just as she did her entire life. The true impact and implications of dreaming as a gift, never resonated in it's entirety until I became saved. Whenever I dream of my mother I have learnt that it is not good. She rarely speaks and it is usually a message or a warning. Thus, when she speaks I have come to realise that I need to stand up, listen, and take notes.

My early Bible reading experience was traumatising as a child and teenager. How I viewed the Bible was very much shaped by how I observed and analysed its uses as I was forced to use it in regular daily Bible Study. For years in my teenage-hood after I had left church I was actually afraid to read the Bible. I remember there were always scary stories with negative connotations linked to misuse of the Bible. One of my older sisters Molly told me about her friend who had gone insane through just reading it. It was around 1976, I was nine and I believed most of the things my siblings told me were factual as the unenlightened youngest and the so called 'Baby'. She said that her friend Wayne who had incidentally become a Rastafarian and 'conscious' as a result. The story goes he had a particular Bible in his possession called the Maccabees which he sat reading, alone, locked up in his house smoking Marijuana. The Bible had apparently driven him mental due to its contents. I have since researched and found that the contents of the Maccabees is seven extra omitted books which would then give the Bible 73 instead of 66 books. The books had been omitted through successive translations but was included in the original King James Version. During my childhood I was always aware and feared the power of the Bible even though I did not understand. I remember how my mother would run to the Bible for everything as though she had a personal close relationship with God and he could be summoned and conjured up in a moment's notice. Mama behaved as though he was on speed dial thus when Mama went to speak to God, we knew do not play around, there will be repercussions and a price to pay.

Now that I am grown in age, life, maturity and Christ, I am thankful that she instilled the fear of God into me very early on. I feel truly blessed to be 'God fearing' and to know that state. The beginning of wisdom for me was to fear the creator. My mother would read her Bible on anyone who in her eyes, "Did her wrong". She would say in her broad Dominican accent, " A-gos-tin-na I givin dem 109 Psalm we", as she spoke Creole a kind of broken French. She would fast and pray and say that she will give it to the Lord. If any of my siblings did wrong she would go and pray and come back with an answer of who did what, how, when and where. Even back then I learnt not to play with the Lord. This year 2013 with all my bible reading it is the first time I read 109 Psalm whilst writing this book and I am no longer afraid and I now know that it is a powerful prayer from King David asking the Lord to help and as we speak to God in prayer she knew he always answer.

I now realised with all of his blessings and God encounters occurring I was definitely in Christ and my mothers Spirit was directing and guiding me but I did not have an intimate relationship with him. Mama guided me back through the Bible and the power of the 'word' nine years after her death through a dream. From that point I have regularly read, studied and applied the word to my life. I now know the Lord has always been with me by my side. There are many times in my life when I have positioned myself into unsafe situations where I could have been killed, but the Lord took me through. I only recognise it now as a follower with spiritual strength and a true understanding of the gospel and the messages it contains, written let us not forget with the hand of the Lord via Moses and a variety of biblical figures. It has always been about me choosing to include him or not. Yes, we all have a choice. The Bible talks about Timothy's early life.

'...Your sincere faith lived in your grandmother Lois and in your mother Eunice...From infancy you have known scriptures'. 2 Timothy 1:5, 3:15 KJV

I have come to believe that Mama shaped and prepared me with a God formed foundation and start in life which serves me today in my journey and walk. In the same way that Lois and Eunice were able to shape Timothy without the help of a Father. Although, my Father was there He worked all the time.

Parenthood and raising my own children who have grown up with me having dreams and as I did they too took it for granted but through education and my walk with Christ I have come to recognition that the gift of dreaming is just that, a gift from God. I attempted to teach my children whom also have the gift of dreaming the scriptures in a way that they could understand giving the words and principles resonance in their lives as they too grew closer to God whilst they are grounded, supported and encouraged in their own journey. I believe that there is a need to give our young a sense of what can be achieved when they harness their God given Spirit and consciously feed their mind and soul with execution and study of the word.

Josephs father Jacob whose name was later changed by God to Israel favoured Joseph for his dreams as he too had the gift of dreams, remember the ladder. Jacob dreamt a vision of a ladder which led up to Heaven and he saw the angels ascending and descending upon it. The Lord spoke to him and told him that the entire land would be given to his seed and they would possess and inherit the earth. Through Jacobs marriage to the two sisters Leah and Rachel whose father was named Laban who was Jacobs mothers brother thus his uncle who gave him refuge after he stole his brother Esau's blessing and birth rite for some bread and lentil soup, also deceived him in the end. The Lord then helped Jacob to triumph over Laban. Between Leah, Rachel and Jacob they gave birth to a nation, the twelve tribes of Israel and as prophesied in a dream sent to Jacob his seed did inherit the earth as they were later depicted and known as the Twelve Tribes of Israel. Genesis 28:29 KJV

Joseph always listened to his dreams, remembered them and spoke of them to his father and his siblings but they did not understand and his siblings heart became hard toward their brother through jealousy. The scriptures show that they were not meant to understand and their hearts were meant to be hard towards their brother as prophesy could not have been revealed. His dreams made his siblings become rivals, jealous of him and it made them despise their own brother. They left him in a pit with no water to be devoured by beast. Then changed their minds because they did not want to spill any of his blood and sold him into slavery instead. He then eventually ends up in prison where his interpreting of dreams gets him to interpret two significant dreams the first gets him out of prison and as far as the court of the Pharaoh of Egypt, where he interprets the Pharaohs dream when none other in the whole land could. He explains that there will basically be seven years of plenty and seven years of famine. Thus he had to be sold into slavery to end up in Pontiphar's house.
Genesis: 37–41 KJV

The Lord had shown Pharaoh what he was going to do. This prophesy had to be revealed with all the test and trails for him to become rich and eventually help his brothers and family years later during the famine. Genesis 42:45 KJV Both accounts serves to illustrate the importance of specific timing in God's Kingdom. Everything no matter how tragic in the flesh, is always for a reason. It demonstrates that the Lord works with specifications. He uses specific people, at specific times, to carry out a specific task or purpose. Preparation has been made before our birth, if we choose to follow we pick up our cross and walk in constant search of purposeful living. Look at the story of Mordecai and Queen Esther, prophesy had to be revealed at specific time, read the book of Esther.

Solomon wrote:
'To everything there is a season, and a time to every purpose under the Heaven...' Ecclesiastes 3:1 KJV

God is truly amazing with wondrous works to perform. Times change, cultures evolve and develop and some would argue